Never Alone

Never Alone

Memoirs of an Identical Twin

HERTHA WILL

iUniverse, Inc.
Bloomington

Never Alone
Memoirs of an Identical Twin

iUniverse books may be ordered through booksellers or by contacting:

iUniverse
1663 Liberty Drive
Bloomington, IN 47403
www.iuniverse.com
1-800-Authors (1-800-288-4677)

ISBN: 978-1-4620-4486-3 (sc)
ISBN: 978-1-4620-4487-0 (ebk)

Printed in the United States of America

iUniverse rev. date: 10/26/2011

Dedication

I dedicate this book to my twin sister Paula , my husband, my children
and their families;
I also dedicate this book to all parents of identical twins, who wonder:
"Shall we let our twins grow up together or separate them at an early
age?"

Acknowledgments

I extend my gratitude to *Barbara Nobel,* who encouraged me to write my memoirs about growing up as an identical twin during and after World War II.

Thanks are also due to Anne Lowenkopf and Maxi Dickinson for many good suggestions while extending the short stories to include early adulthood until marriage.

And last but not least I like to thank my husband for editing and photographic work. Over the years of my writing this collection of short stories, he has been supportive and helpful.

CONTENTS

Preface

Hearing or reading stories about the life of identical twins continues to fascinate many people, and behavioral studies of twins are the subject of great interest for researchers now and in the past.

Questions that are often asked are:

"When growing up together, do identical twins develop more closely similar personalities, likes and dislikes, abilities and intelligence than when they are separated at an early age?" "Do genetic factors generally overwhelm environmental factors?" "Does early separation have a large effect on the similar traits?" "Is it true that identical twins often have the same thoughts at the same time?" "If so, does their ability to effectively communicate with others suffer?" "Should parents of identical twins consider weakening the strong bonds and interdependence that twins often develop if they grow up together?" Is it easier or more difficult in life for identical twins growing up together when they go their separate ways later in life?" And finally and very simply, "Is it fun for identical twins, growing up together?"

Questions like these are frequently asked of me, and I have always found that telling stories about my growing up as an identical twin has created a great deal of interest among children as well as adults.

This has encouraged me to write a collection of thirty-four stories, some funny, some sad, about how it was growing up in Germany with my twin sister during and after World War II. The stories cover the time from childhood, when we swore to each other never to get separated in our lives, to early adulthood, when for each of us, love to a man proved to be stronger than the promise of young twin girls to stay together for ever. And yet, in all these years after we got married, our bond remained as strong as ever, and we still have the same thoughts at the same time, much of the time.

1

Double Trouble

"You don't know who your real father is?" my fiancé asked after I handed him my birth certificate and my parent's marriage license, the documents I needed to get married in Germany.

"It could be somebody you never met. I can't believe your mother kept it a secret for twenty-two years."

Shocked by the question and my own doubts rising in my mind, I looked at the documents again to assure myself that indeed my parents married when I was already six months old. I had to know the truth about my father. Was Tony, whom I loved my whole life, my biological father, or was he not?

My mother came to Munich for an operation in April 1958, six weeks before we were planning to get married. She was in Nymphenburg Hospital, recovering. I needed to know the truth about my father, if only to find peace again. I went to see her to find out from her in person what really happened way back then.

"How are you doing Mami? You are looking well," I said while I handed her a bouquet of flowers and bent down to kiss her.

"Alright I guess. I hate being cooped up here in the hospital. I feel better now and would like to go home. It's so nice of you to visit me again so soon."

"Mami, can I ask you a few questions? Something came up and it is troubling me a lot."

"Sure my darling, anything, just get it off your chest. Tell me what is bothering you?" Mother said, not knowing what she was in for. I handed her the documents.

"Mami. W*ho is my father*? Who is my real, my biological father? Was Toni my father or somebody else? Mami, I need to know the truth now." Sitting on her bed, I saw how her face turned red. She was quiet for a while. It seemed like an eternity to me.

"Why do you need to know now? All these years you twins never asked and I hoped I would never have to tell you. First you were too young to understand, and later I didn't have the courage to bring it up. The situation seemed to be fine the way it was." Exhausted, my mother sank back into the pillows, breathing hard.

"But Mami, I am a grown woman now, about to marry, and I need to know. Just tell me the truth, whatever it is. I can take it. Please, tell me now.

Mother Mathilde

After a long pause my mother told me a story of a time long ago, but imprinted in her memory as if it had happened yesterday.

"I was twenty-one and looking forward to spend my first two weeks vacation from my job with relatives in Dolling, a small town on the outskirts of Ingolstadt. I hardly knew these relatives at the time and felt elated to be invited. Springtime was early in 1935 and the castle terraces were beautifully decorated with bows of fresh birch leafs in honor of Uncle Hans, who brought his bride Elsbie home from Turkey. They were all there for the occasion, Oma Foerster, Hans and his bride, his two brothers Stephan and Karl. I felt so relieved after their warm welcome and was glad to spend some time in this beautiful place. I wondered why my mother hardly ever talked about her cousin and her sons in Dolling. Didn't she like them, and why not? I had to find out from Oma Foerster, knowing very well I would never get an answer from my mother.

Father Toni

"Everybody was busy preparing for the celebration in the evening. I had time to stroll around, looking at the stables with the horses and the moat surrounding the castle, with so many geese and ducks in it. The newly rebuilt white castle was actually a square building with four turrets on the corners and a tree-lined driveway. Suddenly, while I bent down and was talking to the ducks, somebody said right behind me: 'Hello you pretty one.' Surprised, I turned around so fast that I lost my balance and fell backwards into the water. Angry and ashamed I shouted, 'Why did you sneak up on me. Who are you anyway?'

With a sly smile he bowed like an actor and said: 'May I introduce myself to your highness, I am Toni the adopted son of the family.'

"Later that evening at the big dinner party, with lots of wine upstairs in the great hall, everybody was happily celebrating. I loved being there with all the young people my age. You know, I always felt so lonely at home as an only child. Later, there was dancing and Toni walked in, stared at me, and started singing the song, 'Waltzing Mathilda, waltzing Mathilda, you come waltzing Mathilda with me.' Everybody joined in the song while Toni and I danced. He was such a charmer and so good looking. Toni and I danced for a long time, and the world around us seemed to disappear. I fell in love with him right then and there. We had two wonderful weeks together. Every day he found new surprises, and he took me on little adventure trips into the countryside. I never felt happier than during these two weeks in Dolling.

Castle in Dolling with Uncle Hans and Bride Elsbie

"However, several weeks later, when I was home again, I found out Toni had another girlfriend and seemed to have forgotten me. I was so angry about this news, I wrote him a nasty letter, full of accusations. On top of being hurt, I was shocked a month later, when I realized I was pregnant. I felt so embarrassed and hurt that I swore to myself never to tell him. I considered an abortion for a while but couldn't make up my mind until it was too late. I decided to have the baby all by myself. I didn't care to tell anybody and moved to Munich, a city where nobody knew me."

"But Mami, why wouldn't you tell him? Maybe Toni would have liked to have a baby? Why carry this burden all alone?" I interrupted my mother's story emphatically.

"I was young, proud and stupid. I knew your grandmother would not understand and would not forgive me. Never getting along with my stern, old-fashioned, puritanical-minded mother and not wanting to burden my sick father, whom I loved very much, I decided not to tell my parents. I moved to Munich, rented a room, found a short-term job, and spent seven months in the city."

"With little money and feeling ashamed, I didn't go to a doctor till the very last minute. When he told me I was pregnant with twins, I was shocked and overwhelmed with this unexpected news. I walked home in a daze and couldn't think of anything but the dilemma I was in.

"Next morning, my labor pains started and I hurried to this hospital, where we are now. After long hours in labor, I finally delivered twin babies at noon the next day. I couldn't believe my eyes, identical twins, born only five minutes apart. I was so exhausted and felt paralyzed, I couldn't think about the future."

"I chose the name Pauline after Aunt Paula, the only person who knew of my troubles, but I couldn't think of a name I liked for the second baby. So, when the priest came to baptize my baby twins a day after their birth, as it was customary for premature infants, I had no name for you. Hertha was the name of the lady in my hospital room. I liked the name, and so I baptized you by that name. But these things I had told you before."

"They kept my premature babies in the incubator for a month. Meanwhile I had to get my troubled situation in order. I couldn't stay in Munich and I couldn't keep my job. There was no way out. I had to go home, no matter how ugly the scene would be with my mother. You two girls were so cute and looked so much alike, I couldn't give you up for adoption. Finding myself in such a dreadful situation, I finally made up my mind to go home with my two babies just before Christmas. What a present and surprise it would be for my mother, wouldn't you say so?"

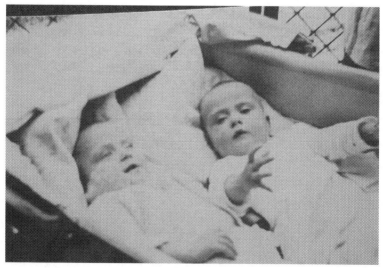

The Baby Twins: Hertha and Polli

"At home, my father was very sick and glad to see me, even with the babies. Before he was dying I promised him, I would tell Toni about my twins. At the time, my mother was surprisingly nice and helpful, although she never forgave me for my mistake. Still angry with this Casanova Toni, I wrote him a letter telling him about his two little girls. He came right away to see his twin daughters. He embraced me and wondered why I never told him before. Toni declared his fatherhood at the city hall, and we married some months later."

Dazed, I sat there at my mother's hospital bed for a while, thinking about my strong-willed mother and what she must have gone through at the time of our birth.

"What a story," I concluded, still in thought. "But Mami, why didn't you tell Polli and me before? I believe you. I really do, and I am so glad Toni is my real father. I am sure Polli will think the same when she hears your story and the explanation, that no man would marry a woman with two babies if he wasn't their father."

2

Our House in Solnhofen

After my parents married, they spent several months in Regensburg at the construction site where my father helped building bridges for Hitler's Autobahnen. Then, our family moved back to Grandmother's house in Solnhofen. Mother needed help with her two little babies. At the time, we lived on the second floor of the spacious house, and Grandmother lived downstairs. During the first years of our lives, we twins slept with our parents in their bedroom. It was a corner room facing east and south, with three six-foot tall, double-pane windows. The two inner walls of the bedroom had two high doors with an opaque window above the wooden door. One of the doors led into the kitchen, the second door opened to a long windowless hallway. The bedroom had green wallpaper, and the windows were decorated with bottle-green drapes and white lace curtains. It was furnished with an oak king-size bed, two nightstands, a dresser, a vanity with a marble top and our baby cribs.

We twins had ivory-colored, wooden cribs with high solid end panels and lower slatted sides. Polli's crib stood at the foot of our parent's bed. Actually, their bed at the time consisted of two separate twin beds, hooked together at the wooden frame.

My father Toni continued working in Regensburg about seventy miles away and came home only on weekends. Tony was a good-looking, dashing young man, who loved excitement, women and powerful engines. Almost every weekend he came racing home on another motorcycle he traded in for the former one. When our parents had a disagreement, as it often happened during the first years of their marriage, Father did not come home for the weekend. Instead he went mountain climbing with his buddies in Austria's "Wilder Kaiser," one of the most dangerous mountains to climb in the Alps.

Mother later told me she felt lonely during these weeks and lonelier on the weekends when Tony didn't come home. It wasn't the life she had dreamed about. On one of these lonely weekends, our baby cribs were moved back to the bedroom. We twins were her only company, her love, her enjoyment and her double trouble.

Our House in Solnhofen

3

Feeling Unloved

When we twins were about three years old, I heard my mother say to a visitor, "Having twins the first time around I wouldn't wish on my worst enemy." The woman visiting that day was five months pregnant and very big for her time. These were the days before ultrasound testing, and she asked my mother to find out, how hard it is to have twins.

At the time, when I overheard this part of the discussion, I concluded our mother must not love us twins to make such a remark. I was shocked and felt sick and barely found my way back to bed. Crying and upset, I couldn't go back to sleep. I got up and woke my sister Polli and told her what I had just overheard my mother say.

Polly was taking the daily afternoon nap in a separate room, so we couldn't talk with one another. At three years of age we both thought we were too grown-up for afternoon naps-a babyish thing to do, we thought. However, our mother needed the rest and some quiet time during the afternoon hours.

We were proud to be identical twins and at that time thought we were the greatest kids on earth. People said how cute and pretty we were, and we liked to believe them. Being twins was so much fun, it never occurred to us that it was not so much fun for our mother and our father. We loved our parents and regretted that our father came home only on weekends from the construction site in Regensburg. We kids assumed our parents loved us too.

Now, all of a sudden, we thought it wasn't so, and were shocked and upset over the terrible news. Heartbroken, we both sat in one of our little beds, with tears running down our cheeks. We didn't know what to do. We couldn't sleep anymore. We felt we couldn't stay in the house any longer with a mother who didn't love us and a father who rarely was home.

We liked being twins, and we wanted to stay together forever and ever. We decided to leave home, but we didn't want to part from our toys, not the ones that were dear to our heart. We felt so sad and needed something to love, to hold close. We packed our most beloved doll, Lola, the old bleached teddy bear, our puppet, Kasperl, and the green alligator in a little wicker toy carriage and quietly sneaked out of the house. We were so sad and determined that we forgot to be afraid. We didn't know where to go, nor did we have any idea what to do. We just knew we had to go away from parents who didn't love us, and we knew we would always stay together.

Taking turns pushing our toy carriage, we walked down the road, through the center of our little town of Solnhofen and out on a dirt road which led us through fields of wheat and meadows of high grass. All the while nobody seemed to notice us two little girls alone. We walked and walked until we were too tired to go on. We never thought we would be missed back home. That thought never crossed our minds because we were so convinced our mother didn't love us. All this time tears kept running down our cheeks, and we could hardly see where we were going. Exhausted, we sat down in the grass on the roadside, hugged each other and cried ourselves to sleep.

Meanwhile, our mother had frantically searched for us in every corner of the house. She together with the visitor and our grandmother asked around in the neighborhood. When they couldn't find us there, Mother became very nervous and afraid. Why didn't I check up on them more often, she told herself. Then the neighbors joined the search through the town, asking every person they saw. Nobody had seen us. Finally, after more than four hours of desperate searching and heartache, she asked a young farm boy who came home from the fields. He thought for a while and then hastened to say, "Oh yeah, I saw two little girls with a toy carriage walking outside of town near the cemetery." Mother and some neighbors following her ran out of town towards the place the boy described and found us there in the tall grass like bird chicks in a nest. Relieved and overjoyed, our mother lifted us up and hugged and kissed us for a long time. After we both explained, with a quivering voice full of joy, why we had left, she assured us of her love and hugged and kissed us over and over again. When Father came home on the weekend and heard about our running away, he hugged us both and made sure to show us his love by playing with us for a long time.

For many years, we heard this story being told to family and friends, and they always ended with the old German folk song, "Haenschen klein, geht allein, in die weite Welt hinein . . .", changing it to fit the story into "Zwilling klein, gehn allein in die weite Welt hinein . . ." (little twins walk alone into the wide world).

Whenever we heard this story, we felt ashamed for what we had done. At the same time, we were so happy our parents did love us, still loved us, even after our stupid adventure of running away.

4

A Heroic Deed

"I am so bored looking at the old clock. Its hands are so slow, they hardly move at all. It's boring and dumb waiting for the time to pass." Whispering these words to my twin sister Polli, I slipped under the blanket.

"It's not time yet to get up from our nap. The little finger on Grandma's clock is only at the number three. We have to take a nap till four o'clock." Polli, my five minute older sister, reminded me of the rules.

At four years, we found it degrading to take a nap every afternoon, thinking we were too old, too grown-up for napping. We felt napping time was a torture. Often we couldn't sleep. Lying awake, I always watched the clock as its hands moved ever so slowly from minute to minute. One hour seemed too long; three hours felt like an eternity.

Ever since we were caught talking with one another, Polli and I were separated. Polli took her nap in Grandmother's room, and I had to sleep on the couch in our living room, facing the clock on the wall whose chimes had been turned off. Often, I got up quietly and sneaked into Polli's room, two doors down the hall.

One afternoon, while tiptoeing to Polli's bed, I heard someone talking to our mother in our live-in kitchen. "Mama has a visitor!" I whispered. "I think it is the old farm woman from the village near Weißenburg. When I came by the kitchen door, I smelled the malt coffee. I'm sure she brought some baked goodies. I only hope there will be some left for us when we are finally allowed to get up."

"Don't be such a worrier," Polli whispered back to me. "Mami always makes sure we get some of the cookies or cakes. Remember, sometimes guests even bring a separate present for us kids."

13

"I wish we would get two presents instead of just one for both of us. I feel we are always cheated by getting only one gift."

"But we get a bigger present most of the time," Polli argued. "Be quiet, Hertha, or someone may hear us and we won't get any present or cake."

We snuggled up to one another and waited impatiently until the clock on the nearby church tower struck four times. With one big leap we jumped to the cold floor and ran barefoot out the door in our pajamas, while holding hands. We were eager to see who the visitor was and if a gift was waiting for us.

It was one of Grandmother's cousins from Dettenheim, a farmwoman who had brought us some whipping cream and "Kupfkissla" for the holiday coffee hour. (Kupfkissla is dialect from Northern Bavaria for little deep-fried yeast squares). We kids loved these "Kupfkisslas," and we liked the "Kirchweih Kuechla" even more. (They are little cakes tasting like American Indian bread in a six-inch round shape with a papery thin middle.)

It was the day of the annual "Kirmes," or "Kirchweih, the church's consecration. A Kirmes, or parish fair, was a big holiday in those days. An old tradition like that couldn't be wiped out so easily among the country folks, not even by a despot like Hitler. A "Kirchweih Kuechla" was prepared once a year for the annual holiday and the consecration of the eight hundred year old church.

Polli and I looked at the delicious food at the coffee table and could hardly wait until some was offered to us. Any cake was a luxury for our family in 1940.

The old woman looked up from her food and started laughing. "Look at these two girls in the doorway with big hungry eyes and runny noses. Oh my God, they are still sucking on their pacifiers like babies. Just look at them, Mathilde; it's so funny, ha, ha, ha!" The farmwoman was so excited she couldn't stop laughing. Bending over with a bright red face she started to cough. "See what you did to me you two big babies."

Ashamed of being laughed at, we turned around and went to the upstairs bathroom to be by ourselves and cried. We loved our "Schnullis," our pacifiers and didn't want to give them up, not even for those delicious cakes waiting in the warm kitchen.

Standing barefoot on the cold floor, we were oblivious to our surroundings. Unhappy and torn between our strong urge to keep our pacifiers and an ever-growing feeling that we had to get rid of them.

Standing there, we kept wavering back and forth. After a while, Polli took me by the hand and we walked slowly to the big toilet seat. We knew what we had to do. We didn't want to be laughed at and called babies again. Without any words spoken, we lifted the heavy wooden toilet cover and looked down into a big, black gaping hole. Looking down into this dark endless pit, we lost our courage.

After a minute Polli commanded, "You do it first! Your "Schnulli" is so chewed up, it must go first!"

With tears in my eyes, I threw my beloved pacifier down the gaping hole and felt like being sucked down myself. A second later, Polli's "Schnulli" followed mine. First, Polli filled the big ladle from the pail next to us and flushed the toilet, then I followed her example, making sure our beloved pacifiers wouldn't be stuck somewhere on their way down.

Speechless, we looked at each other, with tears streaming down our cheeks, veiling our sight. What did we do? How would we ever be able to fall asleep again without our "Schnullis"?

Slowly, we closed the heavy lid to the hole and with it a chapter of our early childhood. We felt sorry for our loss, but at the same time we felt so proud of our heroic deed.

♪

Jacob the Babysitter

Max Fuchs was an ardent stamp collector. He exchanged rare stamps with people from all over the world. At night, our uncle Max held long conversations with other stamp collectors on his short-wave radio and often traded or bought stamps. One day in 1933, he received a special shipment from South Africa with the requested stamps and a present.

What a surprise! The present turned out to be a colorful young parrot. Tante (aunt) Marie and Onkel (uncle) Max called the bird Jakob, a typical name for a "Papagei" (parrot) in Germany. Jakob became the biggest joy in their lives, the replacement for a child they had always wanted to have and never had.

A few months after Jakob's arrival, a special trainer from the famous Frankfurt Zoo came upon request to teach the parrot how to speak. The man spent a week in their home. He tried all the tricks he knew; yet, the bird would not utter one word. Jakob was unusually quiet. He made no sound. He wouldn't even whistle when his favorite food was served. Disappointed and exhausted, the speech specialist bid farewell to Tante Marie and Onkel Max, telling them to continue using his teaching methods. Just at the moment when the man was about to leave the house, opening the door, Jakob whistled and spoke his first words so clearly: "Druck di! druck di!" ("Get lost, get lost!"). Ever since, Jakob continued to speak or mimic other people, but only when he felt like doing so.

When Polli and I were four years old, Jakob was already a wise old bird. Onkel Max died in 1939 and Tante Marie moved into our house. We children loved Tante Marie. She could be very funny and knew how to tell interesting stories from the "good old days."

Jakob, the Papagei, became our babysitter and the upstairs balcony our playpen. The art nouveau wrought-iron railing was four feet high by eight feet wide. The railing's three outer sides were covered with broad-leafed vines, making it a cozy hiding place. High up on the left side of the balcony door was Jakob's place, a wooden bar fastened to a metal grid on the outside plaster wall. Jakob liked it up there. He could watch us, and at the same time observe all the activities on the street below.

Jakob loved to sharpen his beak, not only on the wooden bar where his right foot was chained, but also on the plaster wall. He poked deep holes into it and the mortar, and yellow sand from the wall sifted down to us on the balcony floor.

"Let's make yellow sand cakes in our little cookie forms," my sister Polli called out in excitement.

"Let's spit on it to make it nice and smooth," I replied enthusiastically. We twins scraped up the yellow sand, wet it and packed it into our little metal toy forms. We set them on top of the bench to dry in the sun, all neatly placed in a long row.

A little while later I heard Polli saying, "The cakes are all done. Now we eat them. You Hertha, you eat first!"

With some hesitation I started to poke out the sand cakes from the forms and began to eat them. They didn't taste bad. Polli followed my example, and we ate all the crunchy sand cakes. Mother however, worried we would develop some health problems from all the sand we kept eating.

The pediatrician calmed Mother's mind at the next check-up, "Mrs. Birkl, there is some good in every bad thing. You couldn't get the twins to stop eating the yellow sand cakes, but, as you can see, it didn't harm them. It was even good for them. Now they no longer have any calcium deficiency. The small amount of rationed milk you can buy now-a-days could never accomplish what the yellow sand and mortar did."

The parrot was again allowed to be with us out on the balcony, and we were happy to have our beloved babysitter back. Mother didn't think Jakob was the best babysitter, but she had no time for babysitting, and no one else was available. We children loved Jakob, the funny talking bird. We screamed for joy when Jakob called out, "Hue-hott," ("giddy up") as soon as neighbor Neugebauer's horses started galloping down the steep hill with a bouncing wagon, and a shouting farmer behind them.

One day Polli and I played "laundry day" out on the balcony. We pretended to wash our doll's clothes. Hanging my favorite doll Lola's dresses out to dry, I stepped on top of the wooden bench and reached over the railing to grasp a nearby branch of the tall pear tree. As I bent over, I lost my balance, and fell off the balcony. Luckily, my dress became entangled on one of the big cut off branches of the tree. I still remember seeing myself hanging from that big branch stump. Polli, not realizing the danger I was in, was laughing loudly over the funny sight: Her sister hanging from the tree like the pear next to her. But smart Jakob saw the danger and called out as loudly as he could: „Hilfe, Hilfe!" (Help, help!)

Polli joined Jakob by screaming as loud as she could and ran to Mother for help. "Hertha is hanging from the pear tree. Mami, come! Help!"

When I heard Jakob and Polli scream and call for help, I became afraid too, and joined in their screams.

Our nice neighbor Neugebauer, carefully plucked me from the tree, standing on a high wooden ladder.

Jakob, our good babysitter, had a special treat in the evening, a big portion of his favorite pecan nuts. These nuts don't grow in Germany and were an expensive rarity in the early war years.

One night during the winter of nineteen-forty, we all awoke to Tante Marie's loud wailing cries. Mother hurried downstairs. We girls followed silently behind her, barefoot and cold.

Tante Marie, still in her nightgown, hair loose and messed up, cried and muttered to herself, "Armes Vogerl! Es tut mir ja so leid, aber ich konnte keine Pecans mehr bekommen." ("Poor little bird, I'm so sorry, but I couldn't get any more pecans.")

We children slowly realized something dreadful had happened. We joined Tante Marie's wailing by crying as loud as we could. Why, what's the matter, we wondered. What did Tante Marie mean with crying out I'm so sorry . . . Mother had left to find some tranquilizers for Tante Marie. We couldn't ask her. Tante Marie didn't even see us in her grief. Standing in Tante Marie's kitchen we stepped on a chair so we could look into Jakob's big wooden cage, hanging from the wall. Inside was a little bird strange in appearance with wet and ruffled feathers. The bird was lying on its side, so quiet and still. Could this thing be our Jakob, our friend? Polli and I didn't want to admit the shocking reality. We stood in front of the dead bird's cage and muttered tearful prayers. "Dear God, let Jakob get up again! Please dear God listen to us!

Next day Tante Marie staged a beautiful bird funeral. She laid Jakob on tissue paper in an old shoebox. Polli and I helped her cut out roses from some scrap pieces of leftover wallpaper. We placed the paper roses around our dead friend before going to the woodshed to bury the parrot. Tante Marie had dug a hole in the loose dirt and sawdust, because outside in the garden the earth was hard and frozen. Her music box next to the little grave played an old children song: "Winter ade! Scheiden tut weh!" ("Winter, good bye! Parting does pain!").

Tante Marie told us about the "Bird Heaven in Africa," where Jakob will be playing happily with all the other birds and parrots among beautiful flowers and lush plants. "There will be no cold winters and Jakob can eat all his favorite nuts, as many as he likes. He will be happy. He will treasure all the good memories of his days with us. So now, dry your tears, I don't like to see any more sadness in your eyes. I want to see you both smiling and happy."

Jakob's death was the first big loss of a loved one in our lives. Few years later, heavier losses would come. We had experienced sorrow and learned to understand and cope with death and the facts of life, the tragic, as well as the happy ones.

6

Storytelling

During World War II, most members of our family lived in our house. Grandma, Mother and we four children lived upstairs. Grandmother's sisters, Tante Paula and Tante Marie lived in the rooms downstairs. We twins were now just six years old, our younger sister one year, and our brother was a baby.

The time of nightly air raids on the Bavarian cities had started, and we endured curfews with power blackouts at night. Almost every night, we heard the deep, monotonous sounds of American bombers overhead and cold shivers ran down our spines. The bomber squadrons were heading south to Munich. Our town was located almost midway between Nuremberg, fifty miles to the north, and Munich, seventy miles to the south.

Everybody in the house ran to the windows and watched how the sky lit up above the cities and turned from dark to bright yellow and later to orange and red. Sometimes we imagined we saw the anti aircraft guns shoot down airplanes over Nuremberg. When the planes flew overhead, Polli and I were scared every time. We thought the bombers might drop a bomb on our small town by mistake. I was constantly looking up to the sky, cold and frightened.

To get our thoughts away from the dangers of war during the dark nights of curfew and power-outage, everybody assembled in the only heated room upstairs and told stories. Polli and I liked Tante Marie's funny stories best, especially when she told of things we twins had done when we were little kids.

Tante Marie had a longstanding migraine headache and a deteriorated hip. She often acted like a martyr and seemed to believe it to be true. Tante

Marie indirectly ruled the whole house and all the families living in it. Her handicap, her illness, was her power tool. Everyone was constantly being reminded of her terrible pain and her sleepless nights. One had to adhere to Tante Marie's rules. Usually Tante Marie had a soft melodic voice, but it changed drastically when she had her migraine headache or her hip pain.

She reminded us children about the house rules almost daily. Children have a short memory for rules, especially when they are having fun. Our greatest excitement, playing games up in the attic, was stopped dead when we heard the door slamming downstairs and Tante Marie's angry, penetrating voice ringing upstairs into every corner of the house.

"You will be my death with your terrible noise! What a constant torture! You'll bring me to my grave, you heartless children!" After these whining shouts plus more undecipherable mutterings, we heard the door being slammed shut. For a few minutes we children were quiet and only whispered to one another, until we forgot again.

These outbursts however, didn't keep us from loving Tante Marie when she was feeling good. She kept the most interesting things in her room, stuffed with furniture and mementos. There was a big pink teddy bear with silky fur and a music box in his belly sitting on the couch, waiting for us children to play. The dried skin of a cobra hung from the wall next to the stove. "Why do you keep that awful snake skin there?" I asked Tante Marie.

"To keep it dry and cozy, for this snake came from Brazil, where it's much drier and warmer than here. This skin was a present from our minister of the Lutheran Church when he returned from his missionary work in South America," Tante Marie explained. This was a token of his admiration we assumed. Polli and I knew, although he was married, he visited Tante Marie quite frequently. What an ugly present, I thought, while staring at the lifeless snakeskin. Tante Marie also had many interesting picture books we were allowed to open and enjoy. She didn't mind us asking questions, except when her migraine headache started. We girls knew then not to keep asking any more questions. At that time we were no longer allowed to touch Mother's good books, after we scribbled and drew little figures on the white pages for lack of any drawing paper. Paper and children's picture books were rare during the war years.

Tante Marie had more time for us twins than our mother and grandmother. She understood children. She was fun to be with, when she didn't have her migraines. After kindergarten, we spent hours with Tante

Marie in her room full of things, listening to her stories of a world long ago and so strange, so incomprehensible to us.

Once she told us, how excited everybody in Solnhofen was when the first airplane flew over the town in 1910. She said, "I ran with all the kids and adults out into the streets, shouting excitedly and laughing while the plane made circles overhead." Polli and I loved to hear Tante Marie's funny stories, especially the one when she took a train ride and a farmer brought the goat he just bought at the market into the carriage. "And what do you think that beast did?" Tante Marie asked, looking expectantly at us girls. "You two guessed it. I see it on your smiling faces. That goat made her business right there on the floor between all the passengers. We all had to sit in this terrible smell and wait till we could get out at our stop. Do you think, the farmer cleaned up the mess? Oh no, he sat there and smiled a nasty smile at everybody."

On other evenings, the whole family, with the exception of our small sister and brother, was listening to Tante Marie's stories. I remember us all sitting in the dark balcony room one night during a blackout. The silvery moonlight flooded the whole room. One could almost read a book. Grandma, Mother and Tante Paula were sitting on the tiled hearth, surrounding the tall, white-tiled stove. Their backs were pressed against the stove, soaking up the warmth. Polli and I snuggled up to one another on the sofa, while Tante Marie sat in her favorite rocking chair and told stories of the "good old times."

Listening to Stories

Her two older sisters, Tante Paula and our grandmother, Reta, burst out laughing when Tante Marie told stories about her childhood in the first decade of the century. They smiled and said, "We never saw it that way," or they added, "we have forgotten all these things, but now we remember them again." When Tante Marie told the coffee bean story, all the adults couldn't stop laughing. She described how her family experienced real coffee for the first time and ended her story with the punch line, "We didn't know what kind of beans they were and cooked them for hours."

"Funny you can remember it all so well, Marie," Grandmother remarked in a soft and doubting voice.

Polli and I preferred more recent stories. Since we were six years old, we sometimes were allowed to stay up late with the adults. We loved to be included in these cozy hours of half-light, when the dark night slowly descended. Full moon nights were our favorites. "Tante Marie, please tell us a story about the time when we were young kids!" Polli and I begged.

"Next time when only the three of us are together, I will, but now let's all sing songs about the moon." Tante Marie replied.

Tante Marie, the eternal romantic, recited some poems to the moon, some of her own or those known to other moon lovers. Mother always concluded with a few songs with the texts from Germany's greatest poet,

Johann Wolfgang von Goethe. She either recited them or sang with her pretty voice. We children knew these songs from her and sang along. Mother had played them on the piano and sung them with us when she had some time to spare. Yet on this moonlit night in our balcony room, with all the loved ones around us, it was so much more idyllic, so dreamlike, to sing these songs to the moon.

The next day, we twins had not forgotten Tanta Marie's promise to tell us some stories about us. "Please, Tante Marie, tell us the story about Hertha's accident when she was potty training! Please tell us," my sister Polli begged in her nicest way. I agreed, although I would have preferred a different story. "Please, please Tante Marie, tell us the story when I fell off the balcony! Please tell it again Tante Marie!" I asked when she was finished with the potty story.

How could Tante Marie not yield to our begging? She built up our anticipation and tested our patience by finding some strange excuse or claiming to have forgotten just the stories we wanted to hear. We helped her to remember by starting the stories ourselves, feeling very proud to do so. Satisfied, when she began to tell a story, we blissfully listened to her telling us the stories we had heard several times before and were never tired of hearing again.

7

My Introduction to Philosophy

In September 1941 our father was drafted to the Russian front. Our mother was nine months pregnant. When her time came, we two six year-old identical twins were taken care of at two different places. My sister Polli stayed with Grandmother in Solnhofen, and I was allowed to travel with Grandaunt Paula to her brother's family near Leipzig. Since we twins were separated for the first time more than just a few hours, part of my heart was sorry to be so far away from Polli, and the other part was all excited about our trip to Saxony. Imprinted in my memory are impressions of my first train ride and my first stay with another family that had such different customs from what I was used to at home.

Tante (aunt) Paula and I wait at the railroad station in Treuchtlingen for the express train to arrive. I feel so strange without Polli, but I am glad I was chosen to go on this trip. People are not looking at me, as they normally do when we identical twins are together. I guess a half twin is not so interesting as a pair of twins. Grown-ups like to play the twin game. Who is Polli? Who is Hertha? Most of the time people guess wrong. Only when they trick us and get us to laugh, the more observant among them can tell, because Polli has a dimple on her right cheek and I don't. We like to keep it a secret, for we don't want to spoil their fun. I am actually glad people don't pay attention to me at the railroad station. I am really tired of this twin game adults like to play with us. It makes me feel like a circus attraction, a clown trained for the amusement of others. Now, on this trip without Polli, I don't have to put on an act, and I can hardly wait for what exciting things I will see. Tante Paula is a great pal; she tells me so many interesting things of the places and people I will meet on this visit to our relatives.

"Here comes a shiny burgundy red train!" I shout: "Tante Paula! Tante Paula! Look at the locomotive! It doesn't blow steam as the ones we see at home. I can't believe they are so shiny and clean. Look, the wagons behind it, they look different too," I shout full of excitement.

Tante Paula tells me to hurry up or the train will leave without us. She helps me to climb the steep steps into one of the cars. Inside, we walk along a narrow corridor looking for a number. Tante Paula has reserved two seats in a coupé for us. Finally she finds the right number in a little box next to a sliding door with two long windows on each side. Tante Paula tells me, "Coupé is the French name for a compartment, in an express train, called D-Zug. Everything fine and expensive in Germany has a French name." I think the French people must be very fine people. But Tante Paula explains, "For over 200 years all the nobility and other fine German people spoke mostly French. Now you know why we still have so many French words in our language." I decide to become a fine person and learn French when I grow up.

"Look how beautiful this little room is, Tante Paula!" I call out, running into the little compartment. She corrects me, "*Coupé,* and don't put your shoes on the velvet seats." I hop on one of the two opposite couches and kneel on it to be able to look out the window while Tante Paula heaves our suitcases up on an overhead rack.

The train starts rolling out of the station without our noticing, so soft is the ride. A bump, bump sound gives a nice rhythm; it's almost like music. Outside the window everything is flying by so fast, I can hardly see what it is. There are farms, meadows and woods zooming by. Once in a while I see a river or a city. After a while I find looking out the window boring and think, I want to ask Tante Paula some more questions about our relatives in Leipzig. I have so many questions on my mind, so many things I want to know before we arrive.

Oh no, Tante Paula just started to read a book, and I know I cannot bother her now. I cuddle up in a corner and pretend to sleep while actually I study her face. Tante Paula looks so beautiful and slender in her elegant light-brown travel suit. She is so different from the rest of our blond family. I like her black hair, her dark eyes and tanned skin. Can it be true what Mother said last time when I asked her about Tante Paula's different appearance? With a smile on her face, Mother answered, "You know, the gypsies used to come through town once in a while. They normally steal things when one doesn't watch out, but sometimes they leave a little baby behind. These little children without parents are usually put into an orphanage, or sometimes raised by good-hearted people." When Mother smiled like she did, I knew it wasn't true. I also knew she didn't want me to ask any more questions. Now here in the train I decide, I'll ask Tante Paula herself when she stops reading her book. I know she doesn't mind my many questions. She is always a good sport.

Suddenly, a whistle blows, a loud noise rings in my ears, and darkness falls all around us. I prick my arm to see if I'm asleep. But how can night come without my noticing the sun setting? Tante Paula sees my questioning eyes and explains, "Don't worry, my dear, we are just driving through a mountain in a tunnel."

"But what is a tunnel?" I like to know. She tells me all about tunnels, more than I am interested to hear. Tante Paula tells me I have been sleeping for hours. I missed the city of Nuremberg and the beautiful Saale River, and we will shortly arrive in the big city of Leipzig.

Tante Paula is looking out the window without really seeing what is out there. She continues speaking, softly almost like talking to herself, "Leipzig is a big and very cultured city, has been for several centuries. It was the home of Johann Sebastian Bach with his St. Thomas Choir, and of the world-famous Gewandhaus Orchestra. They call the city 'Little Paris'. Felix Mendelson Bartholdy, another German composer, lived in Leipzig, and Friedrich Schiller, our great writer and poet, wrote his 'Ode to Joy' there. It is also the city of the great German philosophers Hegel, Schoppenhauer and Nietzsche." On and on Tante Paula talks about the city of Leipzig. I am not interested in these great people. I like to hear about my relatives. For the first time, I am going to meet my mother's four cousins and her uncle Gottfried and aunt Hedwig. But all Tante Paula wants to talk about is the greatness of the city and all the famous people, long dead.

She tells me we are going to stay in the great philosopher, Friedrich Nietzsche's birthplace, Roecken. Uncle Gottfried is the pastor of the parish church. Roecken is a small town near Leipzig. "You will like it there; it is a big and beautiful house. But please, don't ask so many questions, and none about Nietzsche when we are there. Uncle Gottfried doesn't like to talk about him, for the man put down God and Christianity. Nietzsche, the son of a pastor himself, turned against everything his family stood for. People later called him the 'Antichrist,' although many scholars today claim he was one of the greatest philosophers ever." Here is that word *philosopher* again, I think. I like to ask about its meaning, but the brakes start screeching, and we roll slowly into the big glass-covered train station of Leipzig.

So many people get off the train now and many more are hustling in all directions on the wide platform. I hold on to Tante Paula's sleeve, for I don't want to get lost. Somebody shouts, "Here they are, our Bavarians!" Suddenly I am lifted up on someone's arm. A woman kisses me on my cheek. It must be Tante Hedwig I think. And the man must be Onkel (uncle) Gottfried; he looks very much like Tante Paula with his black hair and dark eyes. I realize with joy, Mother's gypsy story wasn't right after all.

Everybody is talking at once and I can't understand a word. Do they speak in a different language? I wonder and feel very disappointed. Finally Tante Paula tells me, "It is the Saxon dialect and you'll get used to it." The two tall girls, about 15 and 17 years old, must be Mother's cousins, Irmgard and Waldtraud. They are only interested in what Tante Paula has to say and only give me a short glance. But I am being looked over from top to bottom by four critical eyes. I guess these two boys must be Guenther and Helmut. I don't like to be inspected like this and look away. I make up my mind I am going to show these boys I'm not a sissy, when we are alone later.

We all ride now on a commuter train to Roecken. This train looks very much like the ones back home with a steam engine blowing off a lot of smoke. I look out of the open window of the carriage and enjoy the wind blowing through my hair. The countryside is flat, with wide-open fields, so different from Bavaria.

Roecken is a small town, and we are picked up by a farmer with a big wooden wagon and two horses. Tante Paula explains, "Today, there are no more taxis or private cars for the civilian people. They all were handed over to the 'Wehrmacht' (military) at the start of the war." I like the heavy blond horses with their big hairy feet and sit next to the farmer in front on a wooden bench. All the others are crowded together on improvised seats in the back of the wagon. But as soon as the horses start trotting the animals are farting and their tails swoosh back and forth so close to my nose. I turn my head away and the farmer laughs saying, "This is farm-country, my little one."

Finally we arrive at the stately parish house next to an old gray stone church. We enter a big hallway with a wide stairway stretching up to the second floor in a half circle. The room is flooded with light from an upstairs window. To the right is a study with a heavy oak desk, lots of old, leather-bound books and a beautifully painted cuckoo clock. The cuckoo opens its door and greets us just the moment we walk in. To the left, a great-looking living room with four windows and antique furniture invites us to enter. I hear the house is declared a historical monument, and the furnishings in the rooms downstairs are not to be changed. I run ahead of the others and enter a huge dining room next to the living room. Behind it, I see a big and friendly kitchen. A cook is fixing the dinner. Her name is Alma, and she is very nice to me and gives me a cookie. She is a heavy woman with a friendly round face. I decide I like her, while I am not so sure about the cousins. The two older girls treat me like I'm still a toddler, while the boys, Guenther and Helmut, try to impress me, acting like bullies. They take my rucksack at the front door and throw it back and forth to one-another. I'm afraid my doll inside will get damaged and shout at them. They laugh at my Bavarian accent, teasing me about it.

Tante Paula and I have been in Roecken now for five days. As the days went by, I got to know my relatives better. I like being in Saxony now. I find it exciting to learn so many new things. I think the Saxon dialect sounds funny, and my cousins call the Bavarian accent crude. We laugh about it, and I learn to understand their different dialect and customs.

Uncle Gottfried is visiting people of the parish every day or spends many hours writing speeches in his study. Once he showed me his study, the cuckoo clock, his big desk, full of papers, and his many dusty and yellowed books. "Now you have seen my room and you don't need to come in here any more. You know, little girl, I need my peace and quiet when I'm working." Onkel Gottfried explained and closed the door behind me.

Aunt Hedi (short for Hedwig) is mostly busy with the household, or visits women in town who lost their husbands or sons in the war. She is a very nice lady with blond hair, tied together in the back, and brown eyes. Tante Paula and I come along on some of her visits. We walk trough the streets of old Roecken while Tante Hedi talks to the mourning women. Friendly people come out of their houses to greet us Bavarians. We must be the talk of the town, I assume, but Tante Paula remarked, "They all like their pastor, our Onkel Gottfried, very much and are interested in his visitors."

The two older Fellner girls go by train to their high school in Luetzen early every morning. They have a lot of homework to do in the afternoon and go out with their friends afterwards. I see very little of them and don't mind.

The two boys come home from school at noon. I think Guenther is already in fourth grade and Helmut in second. They have less homework to do and play with me afterwards.

Every day the whole family eats the big meal at noon in the dining room, with the table beautifully set. Everybody says a prayer aloud together and afterwards we hold hands and wish each other "Bon Appetit." I don't like the Saxon cooking. The meals taste so different from what I am used to eating at home. Once they expected me to eat a pink, sweet and sour beet soup. I preferred to stay hungry and gave most of my share to Guenther and Helmut, and ever since we are the best of friends.

In the mornings Tante Paula and I often went on long walks through town and out to the fields and meadows. One day we took the train to Leipzig. I loved the trip to the big city and to all the famous places. Best of all I liked the zoo with so many beautiful and different types of animals. I could have visited them every day.

Some days Tante Paula leaves the house without me. Being alone in the house, I go to investigate the premises. I like to stroll around in the parish garden with all the herbs and vegetables. From the wide-open courtyard in front of the house I reach the open barn where so many old things stand around. There I like to play in an old dusty Landauer. I love to climb inside the open carriage, pretending to be an important lady of times gone by. I find all this old furniture and other things exciting and plan to tell Polli all about it, when I come home again.

One time the door to the little one-room schoolhouse was open. Uncle Gottfried taught Sunday school there. I went in and sat in the benches and pretended to be in school. I know I will go to school next year. I heard how tough it is in school from the boys yesterday. Bragging, Guenther said, "In school everybody has to learn the same stupid things." I don't mind that. I know, I will love school and want to learn French and find out all about philosophy.

One day, when the big church bell struck twelve o'clock noon, I wandered over to the old churchyard. Somebody had left the wooden door open in the high stonewall surrounding the church. Curious, I sneaked through the little entrance from the parish into the old cemetery and saw a gray old church with a short square tower and a high pointed steeple with a weathervane on top. Old gravestones were covered with moss and some graves were overgrown by wild rose bushes or junipers. There were rusty old metal crosses along the outside wall, and some white marble angels looked sadly down at all the wilderness below. The sunrays filtered through the branches of an old weeping willow.

I turned towards the gray stone church with ivy-covered walls and saw two big black marble slabs covering two graves close to one side of the church, enclosed by a low iron fence. I walked inside and stood in front of the more imposing slab with big gold lettering. It must be the grave of the famous Nietzsche, the man who couldn't stop asking questions about everything, I thought. But why did so many people dislike him? Was it only for raising too many questions? I wondered. His grave looked so peaceful with the sunshine reflecting on the gold letters and the shadow of the willow branches on the black marble slab.

Suddenly I thought I heard a voice saying, "Welcome to the land of philosophy."

Stunned, I was speechless for a moment. "But what is philosophy?" I asked. There was no answer.

Disappointed I turned to leave the cemetery. Looking back, I couldn't see anybody around. I only saw the long willow branches dragging over the iron fence in a steady rhythm.

While I left the cemetery, I decided to read Nietzsche and learn about his philosophy when I would grow up and study in college.

8

My First School Day

Time went by fast, and we identical twins were happy in our close relationship and harmonious togetherness. We didn't know any differently and assumed it would be the same in school.

"Look at the twins going to school with their candy-bags!" we heard old neighbor Kronauer saying to his wife when we passed their house, carrying our big colorful, cone shaped candy bags. "Hello Hertha, hello Polli! Have a great first day in school!"

Hand in hand, we girls walked the one-mile dirt road to the elementary school at the northern end of town. We felt uneasy and scared of the unknown. Our big candy bags didn't fill the void of not having our mother with us on our first day in school. Other first graders where accompanied by their mothers. Our mother had caught an early flu virus and had to stay in bed with a high fever. But, at least, Mother had arranged for Rosa, our nursery school teacher, to meet us in front of the school.

Rosa, who used to be our Nanny when we were little, encouraged us, patted us on the head and tugged on our braids.

"Now you'll be with the big kids. Here are children of all ages in this big schoolhouse. You will love it, with all the new things you are going to see and learn. You'll have many picture books, real children's books with colorful pages. These books are not like your mother's art-books, the ones you love to look at and scribble into them. I know you drew little figures on every empty page in it. Yes, yes, I know about this and many other things, you did. My goodness, look how pretty you look in your new dresses and aprons your mother sewed for you."

Rosa kept talking to encourage us twins while leading us across the wide gravel courtyard towards the big school building.

Meanwhile, we walked in a slower and slower pace, and kept looking at this big white schoolhouse, a two-story stucco building with a row of large windows on each level and a small caretaker's house attached to the side. My thought of having to spend six days a week in this building was discouraging. We won't have Saturdays free to spend with Aunt Marie anymore and listen to her funny stories, I thought.

"Rosa, would you like to see what's in our candy cones?" Polli interrupted the silence in the hope to delay our entering the imposing school building. Having the same thought as Polli I eagerly added,

"We have marzipan balls made from potatoes, glazed candied apples and cookies in our candy bags."

"No, I can't look now. Show me later after school, when I pick you up again. We are already late. Mr. Meier, your teacher, doesn't like tardiness," Rosa exclaimed while rushing up the broad stone steps to the arched wide entrance.

"Oh, thank God, we don't have Mr. Hoegner! Isn't he the strict old teacher who likes to spank children? He spanked our mother when she was a child in his class. I'm glad we don't have him as a teacher," exclaimed Polli.

The front hall was large and dark, with doors on two sides. To the right of the entrance, a wide marble staircase led to the upstairs classrooms, lighted by two big windows. Opposite the entrance was the principal's office with its door open when we entered. The principal, Mr. Wagner, greeted us. "Thank you Rosa! I'll bring the twins to the right classroom. School started five minutes ago."

"But I need to go to the toilet!" interrupted Polli. I added like a loyal twin, "I need to go, too," stepping from one foot to the other.

Laughing, the principal pointed to the big entrance door, "All right Rosa, show them the toilet-house outside in the backyard. Aren't you the clever ones, you two? It seems you like to delay going to school as long as possible." Leaving, he shouted over his shoulder, "Give your mother my best wishes for a fast recovery. Your teacher is expecting you in room number one."

The toilet-house was a one-story rectangular stucco structure about twenty by fifty feet, with two doors on opposite sides of the building, one door for girls and the other for boys. While school was in session, the building was a quiet place. Rosa showed us the ten little cubicles with ten little toilet seats. The washbasins were also small, and the faucets provided only tiny streamlets of water for washing the hands. There were no paper towels to dry one's hands, for paper was sparse and expensive during the war years. Instead, newspaper replaced toilet paper at the time.

"Polli, look at these little toilet seats, all dirty and smelly! I won't sit on them ever. But I really didn't need to go anyway."

Pushed in by Rosa, we entered the classroom timidly. Everyone's eyes were upon us. We felt so awful and wished to backtrack out of the door again. Before we could do so, the teacher, Mr. Meier, came towards us. He was informed by the principal and jestingly remarked, "Better late than never! We couldn't really start class without our twins, could we?" The children who had been eating their sweets out of their candy-bags roared, "No," spitting cookie crumbs around while shouting with their mouth's full.

"So now, let's start the lesson since we are finally complete," Mr. Meier remarked, showing us twins our little wooden benches standing next to one another with our first reading books on them.

Mr. Meier was a tall, slender, friendly man with ash blond hair and watery blue eyes in an elongated pale face. We knew him from seeing him on the streets, like everybody knows everybody in a small town. He was one of the few, forty-year-old men in town not drafted in the war because of his tuberculosis. Most men we saw in those days were soldiers, or were dressed in some kind of uniform. Mr. Meier, wearing civilian clothes, looked very strange to us, especially with a suit that had been turned inside out and carefully mended at the elbows.

Our individual tiny benches were scratched and dented from years of use. The desktop had many ink spots from years gone by. Now, due to the war, the old inkwells were empty, and the children had to use slate tablets in orange-colored wooden frames and chalk pencils.

Our first reading book had a red cover with a picture of a little house, a girl and a boy inside, sitting at a table, reading. Inside the book, I saw on each page a big letter and a picture of an item starting with that letter. A big red apple stood for the letter A, a ball for B and a cut circle for C. Everyone was allowed to take the book home for study. Proudly, we carried our books home to show to Mother, for we had no picture books of our own to this time.

I don't remember much else of the lessons on that first day in school, except that I kept staring at the black hair of the girl in front of me, where I thought I saw something moving.

"Pay attention," the teacher reprimanded me. I tried to concentrate and not look at the girl anymore. Later at home, when I told Mother about the girl, she demanded, "Stay away from her, she probably has lice!" This was not an uncommon occurrence at the time when shampoo and soap were hard to come by.

When the bell rang at noon for the end of school, Polli and I were the last ones to leave the classroom. We enjoyed our first day of school, and wanted to linger and look around some more.

The teacher walked up to us and explained, "Nobody is allowed to stay on after I leave and I do have to go home for lunch. If Rosa isn't coming soon, I'll go with you part of the way. But where are your candy-cones? Didn't you get candy-bags this morning?"

"Oh no," we shouted, "We were in so much of a hurry this morning, we must have left them in the toilet house." we twins admitted, sad and embarrassed.

"So, you didn't miss your candy-bags all morning? Was your first day in school so exciting?" Mr. Meier remarked, walking us to the toilet-house.

But there were no candy-bags to be seen, not even scraps of our paper cones could be found. With tears in our eyes, we returned to Mr. Meier,

"Don't worry. We'll find other goodies for you, because we can't have a first day of school without some sweets. Can we? But I want you two to remember that you are in school now. Here, you are responsible for all your things and all your actions, every day. Most important to remember is, try never to be tardy."

At School

9

Tante Marie

Tante Marie was a widow with a hip problem that forced her to walk on crutches. At forty-three years of age she seemed so old to us kids. Tante Marie became our part-time babysitter, and we loved to be with her downstairs in her two rooms.

Reflecting back to those years, I see Tante Marie, with her ash blond hair tied in a bun, sitting at a big, heavy oak table with her crutches leaning next to her chair. I see her, a slender woman, eagerly stitching together many layers of fabric over a boot-tree. The table was covered with heaps of fabric from leftover material, and we children loved playing with the scraps of colorful fabric. Tante Marie made warm house shoes for everyone in the family for Christmas. Being handicapped and bound to the house, she helped out where ever she could in our family, by knitting and mending our clothes. There was always a musty smell all around the room. We kids liked it. We thought it was her perfume.

Once in a while she raised her head, sending long, questioning looks at us through her tiny, black-rimmed round glasses. "Is everything all right with you two?" After a while we heard her remark, "Nice to see you like my Wilhelm Busch book. It's actually not for children, but there are no children's books to buy. I see I have two eager readers here." We loved the famous cartoons of Wilhelm Busch, especially the jolly pranks of Max and Moritz, the two mischievous boys in Busch's books, written in the 19th century.

Sometimes Tante Marie got tired of sewing. "I have to rest my eyes once in a while," she remarked as if she had to make an excuse. "Kids, you are in school now, and I think you are ready for stories I have never told you because I thought you were not old enough to understand them."

Tante Marie explained. "We love to hear them," we girls called out in unison.

"I remember one from my childhood here in Solnhofen when I grew up at the other side of town."

"Story time, story time!" we kids shouted and ran to the old worn-out couch next to the warm tile stove. When she came over to us, we snuggled up to her, one on each side. The old, bleached, pink Teddy Bear, with the loose head and the music box in his belly, was allowed to sit on my lap and listen, too.

"When I was your age, things were very different from today. There was no war, nor any airplanes. And imagine, an old steam-locomotive with only a few wagons came through the valley once a day.

"People were different, too. Everybody went to church on Sundays. All the men wore hats and dark suits-the only ones they owned-, and the women still wore their 'Tracht' (the traditional costume of the region). Old Hefelein Mother is still wearing hers on holidays. The original Tracht had a black, long and wide skirt and a dark-blue silk apron over it. A short, black jacket with some silk embroidery was extra special. On the back of their heads, women wore little round bonnets covered with pearls; and from them fell wide, silk ribbons down their backs. It was a beautiful outfit, and I'm sorry it's no longer fashionable to wear it today."

"In those days people drove around in horse-drawn buggies or in large farm wagons. People worked hard all day, the men in the quarries up in the mountains and the women at home with the children or on the farm outside."

"My family was different. Father owned a farm, a brewery and a pub called the 'Adler'. It's the hotel with restaurant across the bridge on the other side of town. We had to sell all our property in the Great Depression after Father died and Mother became paralyzed. Paralyzed means, she couldn't move at all. Can you girls imagine, my mother had to lie in bed for more than twenty years?"

"But Tante Marie," Polli interrupted, making a doubtful face and stemming her hand to her waist. "How could she be in a bed for so long? Didn't she get all stiff and sore?"

"Yes, my little one, you are so right, but all this happened much later. When I was a child, my family still owned the Adler, the brewery and the farm. There was a lot of work to be done with all that property. Father could afford only one 'Knecht' (farm hand), and we children were expected to help with the farm work or give Mother a hand in the house."

"My parents had thirteen children. Nine were still alive in nineteen hundred and ten, and now there is only your grandmother, Tante Paula, Onkel Ludwig and me."

"At that time, I was ten years old, the youngest of them all, and my duties were light. Every day, I had to find greens in the fields and meadows for our rabbits, and I had to clean their hutches, once a week. I was barefoot and it hurt to walk through the fields of stubble, left from wheat and rye after they were harvested. Shoes were handed down from child to child and worn only on special occasions, on holidays and Sundays."

"Oh Tante Marie, today our shoes are also handed down to our younger sister Bibi because Mami can't buy any new ones in the war."

"You are right, Hertha, nowadays everything is hard to come by, and food is rationed since last year. But let me go on with my story."

"Once every month, Father drove with horse and buggy to Weissenburg, our county seat, for some business. He loved to go to the farmers' market on Saturdays. He told us of all the interesting things on display, beautiful flowers, vegetables and many different-smelling herbs and spices. Father spoke of some farmers who grew so much food that they had extra to sell. Sometimes one could even buy unusual, imported fruits, vegetables and spices." There were bananas and oranges, and sometimes there was even chocolate"

"We hate this war!" Polli and I cried out loud. "We have never eaten any of these things!"

Tante Marie consoled us. "But you are young, and this ugly war will come to an end soon. There will be many, many years in your life for you to enjoy all of these things. We all have to be patient and remember how much more terrible it is for our soldiers to risk their lives out there on the front. Think of how many of them have died already!"

10

Weird

During the years of World War II, at an age from four to nine, we heard and understood little of the war reports. However, when a certain piece of music played for a "Sondermeldung" (a special news report), everybody ran to the radio to listen. We children didn't understand most of the talk, but I still remember the "Fuehrer's" screaming voice. Polli and I didn't like to listen to Hitler's speeches and wondered, why does he always shout when speaking to the German people?

Our father had been drafted to the Russian front, and we missed him, as he was no longer coming home, even on weekends. Our mother had to raise us four children by herself during these meager war years when food was rationed and everyone tried to supplement the small rations, they were entitled to, with homegrown vegetables and raise chickens and rabbits to have meat.

In our little town of Solnhofen, most able men were drafted to the war and the ones we saw in the streets were either too young or too old to be drafted. The women filled in the void by doing extra work at home, in the factories and on the farms.

With most of the women so busy, we twins had to do many household chores after having finished schoolwork. We missed the playtimes with Mother, and there was little time for Aunt Marie's storytelling anymore. However, we got used to be alone for many hours during the day and learned to be responsible by taking care of our five-year younger sister and our six-year younger brother. Also, we loved being in the woods, collecting pinecones and branches for heating. We felt safer in the woods than out in the open where we had learned to throw ourselves to the ground whenever we heard the engines of low-flying fighter planes; fear of being shot at was a constant companion when we were out in the open fields or meadows.

All the more we treasured the occasions when we were done with our work and Tante Marie had time to tell us one of her stories. I had never heard of Halloween when I grew up in Germany. Yet, we kids liked spooky things, or liked listening to Tante Marie's scary stories about poltergeists and monsters. She told us the story of Shaky, the poltergeist, who spooked around once every year in the old schoolhouse. So vividly did she tell us the story that we children grew goose-bumps. On Fat Tuesday (the last day of Carnival), we children dressed in costumes and went from door to door to collect goodies, as it was the custom since grandfather's time.

I remember one drizzling, damp Fat Tuesday in February. Polli and I had been out in the cold weather for hours. We twins were dressed as identical magicians, with black capes and black, pointed hats. Too shy to say, "trick or treat," to the people opening their doors, we collected only one apple and a few nuts in our bag. We were hungry, but so were many people at the time in Germany, and handouts to children were meager.

"I've had it! It's so stupid to go from door to door asking for treats; it's not worth the effort," Polli complained, while chewing on her half of the apple.

"Let's go to Tante Resi! She will be home and always has some goodies for us. Maybe she baked 'Faschingskrapfen' (a donut without the hole and a specialty for Fat Tuesday)." We spent the rest of the afternoon with Tante Resi, our Mother's friend, in her heated live-in kitchen, up on Black Mountain. Our mother was working at a benefit for war casualties, and we didn't like to come home to a cold, unheated house.

When we finally left Tante Resi's warm place to walk home, it was getting dark. We couldn't see the pebbles on the steep path leading through dense undergrowth in the forest and kept sliding and slipping downhill.

"It's your fault we are so late. You didn't want to go out into the cold again and now it's night and much colder yet," Polli complained while hurrying on.

"You didn't like to leave either," was my defense. "Do you think we can find the way home? I'm afraid we may get lost," I muttered, expecting reassurance from my sister.

"Oh yeah, we'll get lost like Hansel and Gretel in the fairy tale. Maybe there is a witch behind a tree or a ghost hovering above in the branches."

"No, I'm not a scared cat. I don't believe in ghosts and monsters. I only like to hear stories about them."

"How about a "Wollperdinger" (Jack-a-lope) you know the big wild hare with the long, spiky antlers?" Polli asked teasingly.

"I know. We saw one hanging on the wall among old Mr. Kronauer's hunting trophies. I'm not so sure about Wollperdingers. The beast looked so real, like all the other stuffed animals he shot. But it's still weird to look at one, don't you think so?"

Meanwhile, we had reached flat ground and entered the wide forest road we knew would lead us home. Relieved, we hurried on, holding hands. Suddenly we heard an owl calling, "hoo-hoo." But was it an owl? It sounded so different, so strange. Looking around we saw two big eyes gleaming in the dark among the spiky, leafless branches "It's a Wollperdinger!" We both screamed, frightened to death. We ran home as fast as we could, splashing through unseen puddles and falling over stones in the dark.

Home, sweet home was an unheated house, but a familiar and safe place on that spooky Fat Tuesday in 1943.

11

The Old Cemetery

The old cemetery as I knew it is gone. Today, in its front part, stands a modern Bauhaus-style structure, the new town hall of Solnhofen. Yet, in my mind, I see the old cemetery of my childhood in war-torn Germany on a cold November day in 1943.

Filled with overgrown graves, rusty metal crosses and some broken head stones, the old cemetery is obviously no longer an active burial ground. The last person was buried in 1925, and a war-memorial for the fallen soldiers of World War I was erected in the same year. In winter of 1943 during World War II, it is a peaceful place, located off the busy streets of our town. Only a few old women, with bent backs from too heavy manual work, visit the graves of loved ones long gone.

In this half-forgotten sanctuary, juniper bushes grow into enormous blue-green thickets, and spiders weave their intricate webs from the pointed cypress trees to the white marble statues. One old grave with a white, peaceful-looking angel, whose bent head is surrounded by spider webs, is my favorite place. When the morning sun reflects in the dewdrops on the spider's silvery threads, the angel's head appears surrounded by a gleaming halo.

The big, black iron gate of the old cemetery is always open. Only three hundred feet from our house, in the middle of a high brick-wall, is this side entrance to our favorite playground and hiding place. My sister and I run down the gravel road from our house to the cemetery gate, skipping over some of the big stones washed out by the last rains.

Some of our six chickens like to lay their eggs under the prickly juniper bushes in the old cemetery. Every day, Polli and I go on an egg-hunt, searching everywhere and looking in and under every bush. Filled with pride and joy, sometimes dirty and with scratched arms and knees, we carry the precious eggs home to Mother. Meat is scarce and instead eggs are used in our diet.

We play house under one of the dense juniper bushes where we hide on old blankets, pillows and boards we dragged down to build a cozy nest.

Mother knows about our secret hiding place; she can keep an eye on us from her kitchen window and thinks we are safe. We think so, too.

Today, we are not in our hiding place. We stand under one of the tall chestnut trees where yesterday we saw older boys high up in the branches, throwing chestnuts while singing the song from the radio, "Bomben auf Engeland" (Bombs on England). Polli and I think it was great and daring to climb up the tree, and today we want to do the same. We know, we are not allowed to climb trees, especially chestnut trees whose branches brake easily. The temptation stands right in front of us and is too hard to resist.

"Polli, Polli don't climb any farther. We are so high already I can hardly see the ground!" I shout, from several branches below.

"Oh, you chicken! Don't be afraid. The branches are so big and strong. They'll hold us. We can even sleep up here, it's so safe." I hear my sister's assurance from six feet above. Pointing to the wide cobblestone street outside the cemetery Polli shouts anxiously. "Do you hear the brass band playing? There is a parade going on with marching soldiers. They are coming our way . . . Oh no, they are coming around the corner into the cemetery."

"What do they want here? Look, they are all dressed up in brown uniforms! These are all SA (Storm Troopers)." My loud voice decreases to timid whispers.

I hear Polli's hushed remark, "Now it's too late to climb down from the tree. We are caught up here. I hope, no one will see us and tell Mother. Hush, hush, keep quiet, or someone will see us!"

In a low voice I reply, "I can't stay so high up on this branch. My place is too hard and painful. Besides, I want to get a better view of the old 'Hünengrab,' (an old Germanic burial ground called a dolmen, built with huge monolithic rocks). Look, Polli, at all the activity at the dolmen, the Veterans war-memorial. The parade stops right in front of it and the brown-shirts form a circle around the big rocks." While I move to a better spot, some chestnuts come loose and drop to the ground near spectators who followed the parade and assembled right below us.

"Are you insane, Hertha? Someone may see us. I don't have a soft seat either. Hush, hush! We have to be very careful."

"Polli, do you see, they are marching in that funny goose-step, and they lift their stiff legs so high? Oh look, these SA people are from our town! I know some of them. And there is the mayor, and there is our neighbor, Mr. Kronauer! Why are they acting so strangely, so differently today? Listen to the songs they sing! These are the songs we heard on the radio during the rally in Nuremberg, just before the 'Fuehrer' gave a shouting speech." Excited and almost out of breath, I whisper, shifting to a more comfortable spot.

"O yeah, I remember now." Polli answers. "Today is Veterans Day, and the Nazi people have to play their act, as Mother would say. Now the band plays again and everyone sings the Horst Wessel song we heard on the radio this morning. I like the melody, but the text is so sad. They sing about a friend and comrade, who died in battle. Why do they sing it here? We don't want to hear about killing and dieing anymore."

"But Polli, it's Veterans Day, that's why they sing this song here at the ancient 'Huenengrab' (Celtic grave site) below us."

"You're right, I forgot, that's what they do, to honor all the dead soldiers, even the ones from other wars, long ago."

"Polli, I can't sit here on the tree branch anymore. I'm hurting all over. When will this ceremony finally end?"

"Be quiet Hertha, I'm hurting too. We have to be patient. Look, in front of the war memorial the mayor gives a speech and lays down three fresh, green wreaths with wide, red ribbons and a black "Hakenkreuz" (swastika) in a white circle."

"Listen, Polli," I whisper, holding my hand in front of my mouth. "Now the band starts playing again and the SA leaves the cemetery and all the people who watched follow slowly."

Cold and stiff, with hurting arms and legs, we climb carefully down from our observation spot. Recuperating in our cozy nest under the juniper bush, we talk excitedly and feel relieved that our big adventure was not discovered.

"We know, we have done something wrong, climbing up the tall chestnut tree. With a bad conscience I ask, "Shall we tell Mother about it? I have so many questions for her. Today, these people behaved so differently from their normal ways. Even Mr. Neugebauer, a nice and friendly man, acted so strangely today, almost like a puppet. I think it is some kind of a game these people play on Veterans Day."

"Let's not tell Mother. You know, she doesn't want us to climb trees." Polli decides for both of us.

"But can we forget the questions about what we just saw?" I ask nervously.

"Never," we both agree simultaneously and know this cold November day in the old cemetery will forever stay in our minds.

12

A Present for Saint Nicholas Day

In November of 1943, winter came early to Germany. Advent is a four-week period of emotional and spiritual preparation before Christmas, an old tradition still observed by many families during World War II and today. The weeks before Christmas were so different from today's big shopping craze. Store shelves were almost empty of goods. What was available of the scarce food supply was rationed and could only be bought with food stamps. Most people in our town of Solnhofen had no meat for the holidays.

Our family was lucky to have two of our rabbits as a holiday roast. A neighbor, old Mr. Stoeckel, butchered the animal because mother didn't have the heart to do it. We twins cried our hearts out when our pets were killed. During the whole year, we girls raised and fed our bunnies. Polli and I grew to love these little cuddly creatures, gave them names and played with them. Hoppy, my white bunny, was very clever. I liked to show him off walking with him on the street without a leash. In summer, we collected greens every day after school for our six rabbits, and during the winter months we fed them with kitchen leftovers, mostly cabbage and potato peels.

The Christmas holidays caused much commotion in our family. Our father was expected to be home for Christmas on furlough from the Russian front. Mother had to prepare everything for Christmas from scratch. She had to organize, plan the meals, craft presents for her four kids and decorate the tree on Christmas Eve. We two eight-year old girls had to help. Mother was a great cook and magically prepared a delicious holiday meal. It was roast rabbit stuffed with apples, with sauerkraut and tennis ball-size potato dumplings as side dishes. For desert, she made a cake with marzipan, which she had made from potatoes as the major ingredient. During the war years, most children were skinny, but had bloated "potato bellies" from eating too many potatoes to fill their stomachs, for lack of other food.

My twin sister and I preferred the four weeks of Advent before the big holidays. It was a quiet time with long hours of twilight and early nights. Our whole family crowded together in the only heated room. Hanging from the ceiling was a freshly made Advent wreath made from balsam boughs, decorated with a red ribbon and four red candles. Only one candle was lit every evening during the first week while we all sang Christmas carols. Every week another candle was lit in preparation for the big holiday of light, Christmas, with the "Lichterbaum" (tree of light) as its symbol. Mother had saved rationed emergency candles all year for this occasion. She melted them to make little candles in a mold to fit into the metal holders, clipped to the Tannenbaum (fir tree) branches.

I remember one particular day in late November when we twins had just finished our homework at three in the afternoon. We went to the window to watch the first snowflakes falling, covering the village with a beautiful white blanket. We both loved to watch this transformation from the drab, gray tones to a fairytale winter wonderland.

We were sitting on the window sill with our legs pulled up, facing one another, with our backs pushed against the side walls and our feet pressed together. An old, knitted blanket from Grandmother's dowry, still smelling of mothballs, protected us from the window draft. Sitting there we felt so cozy and peaceful. Snowflakes melted on the windowpane, forming tiny water droplets that ran down into the snow on the outside window ledge.

Tapping on my knee to get my attention, Polli pointed to the dark line of French POWs drudging through the fresh snow. "See the poor men down there! They don't look happy. Aren't they as glad about the new snow as we are?"

"I guess not" was my answer, adding "look they don't even have good shoes in this cold wet weather."

Polli, her chin in her right hand, the elbow on her raised knees, looked out of the window in deep thought. After several minutes, Polli said the words I was just about to say myself. Typical for us twins, we often had the same thoughts at the same time. We laughed and repeated the words aloud, like an echo coming back double in volume: "Maybe they save their good shoes for the holidays as we do!"

Looking down at these poor men in their worn-out old clothes, with shabby rags thrown over their shoulders for lack of a winter coat, we knew our holiday shoe idea was wrong. We suddenly felt so sorry for the poor men out in the cold. From our second-story window, we could overlook the whole prison yard with about forty dark figures sitting on a stack of wooden boards, while others slowly walked their rounds in the new virgin snow.

The prison property belonged to Stadelbauer, one of the richest men in town. He had the only facility to house the prisoners, his former ware house. The POWs were sent to Solnhofen to work in the limestone quarries up on the hills. Weekends, the prisoners stayed in town and took an afternoon walk in the prison yard. The wide, empty yard was about one hundred by three hundred yards, surrounded by a tall wire fence. An alleyway, bordering on our vegetable garden, used to lead to a back door, but was locked during the prison years.

Two men, usually separated from the other prisoners, paced up and down along the fence of the alleyway. Three months later, we knew their faces well. They looked up and smiled when they saw us sitting at the window. We waved back shyly; we knew, we were not allowed to communicate with the prisoners.

Poking me in my rips, Polli shouted, "I have a great idea. Let's make two little St. Nicholas presents for them. You know, like the Apple Santas we made for Mother last year for Christmas."

"But Christmas is still several weeks away", I said. "Next week is St. Nicholas Day, when we place our boots at our front door and get them filled with cookies, and nuts. It's the perfect day to give the two prisoners each a little Apple Santa. We'll have time to get two beautiful red apples from Oma's (Grandmother's) storage place up in the attic. We have to find nice walnuts, too, some stiff red paper and some cotton from medicine bottles!"

All excited about our great idea, our new big secret, we left the room to look for these supplies.

"I know where Mother keeps the good glue hidden," my sister called out while running to fetch it.

"I know where to find the toothpicks and the cotton balls," I called after her, adding, "But walnuts are a problem. Mother saved some for

Christmas cookies. I know where they are all shelled and ground ready for the next baking day. But we need full walnuts with the shell still on."

"Let's go downstairs to Tante Marie! She will give us two walnuts. She keeps them for Jakob's parrot food. Jakob won't mind. We'll give him two hazelnuts instead." Polli suggested, rejoicing while walking back to me.

"Great idea," I replied, "we need two pretty walnuts, without cracks, so we can draw faces on them with our crayons."

We knew Tante Marie would give us two walnuts if we begged nicely for them. Excited and filled with enthusiasm, we ran downstairs to collect what we needed.

Secretly, we collected all the items. While pretending to do our homework, we built the two little Apple-Santa Clauses. Polli held the pretty dark-red apples while I poked a tooth pick into the top. It was tricky to get the two walnuts to stay on top of the toothpicks. When we finally managed to do it, we cut red paper into two half circles and wrapped it around the nuts to make two cone-shaped hats. We glued them on top of the walnut heads. Carefully, each one of us girls drew faces on the nuts with black and white crayons. To finish the Apple Santas, we pulled cotton balls apart to make beards and glued them to the lower half of the nuts. Proud of our accomplishment, we carefully placed the two Apple Santas into a shoebox and hid them in the woodshed at the back of the house. They were ready to be given to the two prisoners on St. Nicholas Day.

On December sixth, St. Nicholas Day, right after we returned home from our long walk from school, we sneaked into the wood shed. There was our hiding place behind some stacked-up logs. A perfectly safe place for our presents, we thought. The logs would not be burned until the end of winter. Carefully, we lifted the cardboard box from behind the logs. We had placed our two little Santas in it to protect them from dirt and dust. But what did we see?-A big hole in the limp and damp cardboard box. A foreboding of what was to come crossed our minds.

Inside the "safe container," two half-eaten Apple Santas were sadly sitting in the middle of crumbled wood shavings. Our perfect hiding place for the two Santas made a perfect winter home for a family of mice. Shattered by the sight, our enthusiasm plunged to zero.

"That's what we get for doing things in secret," Polli said in a low voice after looking a long time at the disaster. After a while she shrugged off the bad sight and remarked smilingly, "So we made a tasty present for a family of hungry mice."

"But we wanted to make these poor prisoners happy," was my sad response.

"I know we are not allowed to talk to the prisoners. But we can't anyway, because they speak only French, I heard Mother say the other day."

Polli, the more practical one of us twins, had the answer. "We don't plan to talk to the men. We only give them a present to make them feel better. We'll repair the two Santas with the apples we still have left in our lunch boxes. These apples are not as pretty as the others were, but they will do. An apple is an apple after all."

We fixed the two little Apple Santas right there in the wood shed. Under the cover of newly falling snow, we sneaked down to the garden, hiding our presents in our jackets. Underneath the big wire fence, we pushed the two little apple men to the other side. Two little red Santas stood in the snow on the low concrete wall, waiting to be found. The falling snowflakes slowly covered our footprints. Our secret was safe. But would the two prisoners find our little presents? We hoped the light snow would not cover the two bright-red Apple Santas!

Three hours later, we saw the two lonely prisoners bend down to pick up something almost covered by the snow. Each of them held a little red Apple Santa in his hand. They looked up to us. Waving back from our window high above, we were so happy to see their smiling faces.

Apple Santa

Many years later, in the mid '50s, when we came to Solnhofen to visit our grandmother, she handed us an envelope.

"Strange mail you are getting nowadays. Whom do you know in France? The envelope has only a few scribbled words on it." Curious, we stared at the bad handwriting:

To the Twin Girls
Solnhofen, Bavaria

WEST GERMANY

Stunned, we heard Grandmother say, "Can you imagine, a letter from France with so little information still reached you? Thanks to our old mailman, Mr. Auer! He still remembered you when you used to live here ten years ago."

We had the French letter translated for us, because our meager French language ability was not sufficient.

It was a thank-you note from Lyon, France by a Jacques H. Pevaer, telling us how he had planned to write to us for many years. But without any name or address he thought it was useless. His two daughters, of whom he was always reminded when looking at us twins during the dreary days of his imprisonment, encouraged him to write to us anyway. Mr. Pevaer wrote, he hoped his letter would find the right address and he would have a chance, to tell us how happy we made him and his friend Henry Villarde on that snowy St. Nicholas Day in 1943.

13

The Black-Rimmed Letter

Coming home from school we find the house unusually quiet. "Where is everybody?" Polli asks with a questioning look. We know instantly something is wrong. Assuming the worst, we run upstairs as fast as we can, to find Mother. "Mami, Mami what happened?" we scream, pushing the kitchen door open with a loud bang.

Mother sits motionless at the kitchen table with a black-rimmed envelope in her hand. Her face is red and swollen from crying, and she turns her head with no expression in her eyes. When she recognizes us, she bursts into tears and with a choking, hardly audible voice, stammers: "Your father is dead."

Earlier on this day, in March 1944, Polli and I walked to school. Snow has fallen during the night. In the early morning light, we trudge through the deep snow on our long walk. Our feet are wet and cold, and our boots are too tight for our growing feet. We are eight years old and have to wear Grandmother's boots from the time she was young. Mother found them up in the attic among other things from the turn of the century. We hate to wear these old-fashioned high-laced boots, but Mother couldn't buy new ones for us; the shelves in the stores are mostly empty since last year.

Before school starts in the morning, all pupils have to stand outside in the cold courtyard in long straight lines. We have to stand straight, with our right arm up for the "Heil Hitler" greeting, while the "Hakenkreuz Fahne" (swastika flag) is raised. The older kids sing, "Die Fahne hoch . . ." (Raise the Flag). Polli sighs and her look tells me she is as bored as I am about what we think is a stupid act for school children; it is a ceremony that must be performed by adults in many public places at the beginning of the work day. My toes prickle, my feet hurt and I think I can't stand any longer in the freezing cold.

Suddenly the siren's shrill ring disrupts everything. "Fliegeralarm" (air raid). Polli and I scream in shock and run towards the school building, holding hands because we don't want to get separated in the chaos in the school yard. Everybody rushes to the air raid shelter below the big school building. Down in the shelter, we children sit on low, wooden benches, packed together in tight, long rows. We don't feel cold any longer. We are tense, and fear is in every child's eyes. We hear the droning sounds of the bombers overhead. The awful sound goes on and on. It seems endless to us children, cowering in the dark. The cold shelter has a musty smell; its dim, diffuse light comes only through an airshaft. The room, packed full of kids, is so quiet. Nobody dares to speak, everybody is afraid. I think the only sound I hear is Polli's heartbeat, or is it mine? I wonder. Someone cries out, "When will this finally end?" Fear is all around us, like the thick, stuffy air. I embrace my sister while she covers her ears to drown out this awful noise. We both shiver, not from cold but from fear.

When the shrill siren announces the "all clear," we think it's the end of danger and feel so relieved, so happy. One by one, the children emerge from the shelter and the teachers tell them to go home right away. There may be another alarm, or a fighter plane attack, our teacher tells us, explaining, "You know the air-raid in Treuchtlingen happened right after the first bomber squad had flown overhead to Munich." Polli and I grab our satchels, slip into our thin coats and run home. On our way, we slide and stumble on the now wet and slippery snow.

"Polli, your brown lunch bag fell out!" I call after my sister.

"I don't care if it gets wet. It's always the same dark rye sandwich with no butter and only that homemade jam from the pine buds we picked last spring."

At home, we can't believe the awful news of our father's death. Impossible, it must be a mistake. Vati was just here on furlough during Christmas. He can't be dead. Looking at Mami with her tear-stained face, the shock, the tightness in my chest comes back and I have trouble breathing. Polli and I look at each other and simultaneously we know what we want to do. We run to our Mother, give her a big bear hug and cry in concert. After a while, Mother suddenly stops and feigns laughter, "Look at us three cry babies! What a sight. Lucky, nobody is around to see us like this." We admire our brave mother, watching her getting up from the kitchen table, drying her face and telling us to do the same. After straightening her dress she comes back to us, takes us in her arms and tells us, "We all must be strong now, stronger than before. The war is not over. Who knows what will await us in the near future." Looking at the clock she gasps, "O God, I forgot I to pick up Bibi (our little sister) from Kindergarten and Butz (our brother) from our neighbor.

Stunned and numb, we twins remain behind in the kitchen. Minutes pass in silence; I don't know how many. Suddenly I hear Polli scream, "Look at this mess. Mami forgot the sauerkraut on the stove. It's all brown and burned."

Now, I smell the stench of the burned cabbage, too and run to open the windows. Oh, how nice the fresh, clean air feels. The snow in the garden covers the comfrey beets and the fir branches that the wind had blown away from the hardy vegetable. Looking at the frozen things out there, I wonder, is Vati lying under the snow, frozen stiff like the beets? "No, it can't be. No, no, no, he is not dead." I cry out and turn from the window to ask my sister for some confirmation,

"Polli", I cry, "Vati can't be dead! It's only an envelope with a letter, only some words that claim such an awful thing. The letter doesn't even say how he died. We won't believe it till they send him back in a coffin."

Polli interrupts my thought, "Do you know they don't send dead soldiers home in a box from Russia anymore? Mrs. Käfer told me last week, they bury many soldiers in one big grave. It's called a mass grave. Mrs. Käfer never even got a black-rimmed letter, as we did. She thinks Mr. Käfer is still alive and will come home some day."

"So, why can't we think Vati is still alive? We'll pray every night for him to come back to us. God must hear our prayers. We saw Father so seldom all these years. Before the war, he was in Regensburg at the big autobahn construction site and now he is in Russia. Mami said, Russia is much farther away."

"He can't be dead," Polli remarked, slowly adding, "He told us at Christmas when he was on furlough, we shouldn't worry, he'll be safe, he isn't at the front where all the shooting takes place, adding 'You see, my little girls, I am rebuilding the very railroad bridges that the partisans have blown up.'" Vati was so sad during his furlough. We loved to listen to his stories and hoped he would soon come home for good.

"Yeah, I remember when he told us, things were not going well for the German army on the Russian front. Mami got mad at him for telling us so much about it. She always worried some neighbor, or any other person, could be a Nazi spy and hear us kids talk about it later. Polli, can you believe it, Mrs. Käfer told me, there are boys in the Jungvolk" (pre-Hitler Youth, 10-13 year old), who turned in their own parents for saying something that might be negative for the Hitler regime? Their parents' talk at home was often enough for them to get arrested by the Gestapo, and often the parents were never heard of again."

"I can't believe kids would do such a thing and betray their own parents," Pollli remarked in a hushed voice; and added "Mami worried about the spies and Vati didn't. He liked to talk to his family about his experiences, about his fear of losing the war and the uncertainty of what's to come. One time, I remember, Vati had a strange smile on his face when he said, 'It's a scary thought, but I think it's possible that some of these partisans blowing up the bridges are the same people I play cards with once in a while.'"

"And Polli, Vati also told us, he learned to speak some Russian and traded cigarettes with Russisn civilians for food. I still remember him, standing in the living room and saying. "Where from do you think I got the vodka, or the big tin cans with the sunflower oil and the half piglet I sent home last year?' I think Vati really didn't care about the Nazis, or their spies everywhere."

Once he told neighbor Kronauer even in front of the house, "The simple Russian country folks are really not bad people. It's awful we are in this terrible war." Polli do you remember when Mami told him he shouldn't talk like this, someone may overhear his words."

"Yeah, I remember Vati was very sad the whole time he was home last Christmas. Even the holidays didn't change his mood."

"But he smiled when he saw how happy we both were over the doll house he built for us."

"Yeah, I think it was the only time we saw him happy during his last stay with us," Polli slowly responded, while remembering one beautiful holiday moment.

"Polli, can I tell you a secret? It's a secret between Vati and me. He asked me to swear never to tell Mami or anyone else. But Polli, you are my twin sister. I can't keep it a secret from you. We are twins, one and the same, as they tell us. Polli, swear you will never tell my secret to Mami or anybody else. Swear, Polli, 'Hand auf's Herz,' (put your hand over your heart) and swear."

"I swear by God and with all my heart. But please tell me what the secret is? You should have told me long ago. If Vati comes back I won't tell him you revealed your secret to me."

"All right, I tell you. On Christmas Day morning, I ran to the balcony room to hide some of my potato-marzipan so Bibi and Butz won't eat them. When I opened the door of the unheated room, there was Vati standing in front of several liquor bottles, drinking. I knew Mami didn't like him to drink Schnapps in the morning and told him so. He turned around, put his finger to his mouth and whispered, 'Hush, hush-quiet.' He came over to me and said in a low voice: 'Can you keep a secret? It's a secret between you and me. Never say a word to Mami.' I swore with my hand over my heart and felt very proud. Vati lifted me up high towards the ceiling as he used to do when we were little and said, 'That's my girl, that's my big girl who will keep our secret!'"

Polli, I really never told Mami or anybody till now about his drinking. So Polli, will you keep my secret, too?"

For many years, we twins prayed at bedtime for our Vati to come home again. We never saw his body in a bag, a box or a coffin. We couldn't, or didn't want to believe he was really dead. We hoped, our father would one day show up at our front door unexpectedly, like Marie Rose's Daddy came home after two years missing and believed dead.

One evening in 1948, three years after the war ended, Mother heard us twelve-year old twins still praying for Father to come home. She came into our bedroom and sat down on Polli's twin bed next to mine. She looked at us quietly for a long time, and while stroking Polli's and my hair she told us in a sorrowful, soft voice: "Yesterday, I got a letter from a former comrade of Father's in Russia. He described how Father was killed in a fighter attack on the railroad station where he and others were checking out supplies that had arrived on a freight train. Everybody sought shelter underneath the freight cars. When the planes had left, Vati was the first to crawl out from underneath the freight car; but suddenly a single fighter plane returned and opened fire on him. Your father had no chance to survive and died on the way to the field hospital.

So, pray now for your father to go to Heaven. He was not a religious person but a good, decent man. Now we finally have his death certificate. Your father died on March 12, 1944 in Wapnjarka, Ukraine, near Odessa." He will never return to us.

14

Our World of Chickens

Polli and I were eight years when Mother brought thirty cute little baby chicks home from an incubator. We didn't know they hatched from eggs, because we had never seen our hens sit on their eggs much longer than it took to lay them.

With food so scarce during World War II, our family decided to raise and keep chickens to have eggs for our meals. Since we twins were the oldest in our family, we were assigned the job to collect the eggs and take care of the tiny baby chicks.

Every spring, Polli and I cared for about fifteen tiny, fuzzy baby chicks. We loved the little fur balls and built a little chicken kingdom with a flat cardboard box with layers of newspaper and sawdust in it. On one side of the box we attached a smaller cardboard box and painted it like a house with doors and windows. Inside the little house, we piled up chicken feathers to keep 'our' babies warm. Outside the little chicken home, we placed little trees from our toy box to make it look beautiful.

"These stupid chicks have no eye for the beautiful things we gave them! They dirty everything with their smelly droppings. Let's remove all these nice toys and leave them with only a plain box. They deserve no better!"

"You are right, Polli, I agreed. Typically, we identical twins thought the same things, much of the time.

We placed our chicken kingdom up in the attic close to the windows, taking advantage of the little sunshine there was; for the weather is still cool and cloudy in Germany during spring time. We knew babies needed warmth and food. Every morning, before we went to school, we placed our chicken box close to the southeastern window in the attic and in the afternoon on the other window facing west. On rainy days, we kept our chicks in Mother's warm kitchen right next to the big iron stove, heated with firewood. Coal or gas was not available for home heating in Solnhofen during the war.

Every day we went out to collect stinging nettles, which we carefully chopped, while holding the stems wrapped in newspaper, so we wouldn't get stung. The nettle greens we mixed with gruel and egg yolk and placed it on a piece of cardboard in front of the chickens.

Many hours we spent observing the lives of the baby chicks. We studied their habits and their reactions to our rules. We punished the offenders when they behaved against the laws we had put down for their kingdom. We spanked the little chicks softly with a toothpick.

Polli and I realized the biggest, fastest growing chicks were pushing away the smaller ones to get most of the food. They also occupied the warmest spots in the box. This happened every day, and we concluded these must be the male chicks, exhibiting the same behavior as the bullies in our school.

We felt sad and mourned when several of the baby chicks got sick with diarrhea and died. The dead chicks looked so different than before. They looked very pale and shriveled up. For our dead baby chicks we made little graves with crosses from toothpicks in a corner of Grandmother's flower garden; we called the spot our chicken cemetery.

Mother's kitchen was the only warm room in the house, and everybody assembled there in the evening. After the fire burned down in the big iron stove, we placed the chicken box carefully inside the oven. A stick was put across the opening to prevent the door from shutting. Before it was chicken bedtime, all the little chicks were let loose on the kitchen floor. We children improvised fencing by using pillows and overturned chairs, so no chicks could escape. Tante Marie carefully stepped inside the circle among the scurrying little chicks and squatted down calling, "Cluck, cluck, cluck." She lifted her long warm woolen skirt and shoved all the little chicks under it. When some of the little chicks sneaked out from under her skirt, Tante Marie quickly fetched them and pushed them under again. "I keep them warm like a mother hen would do." Tante Marie explained to us. "The poor little babies never had a mother." All the children and some of the adults had tears in their eyes from laughing so hard while watching Tante Marie playing mother hen and the little chicks scurrying around her.

After several weeks, our chicks outgrew their box. The weather became warmer, and they could stay outdoors in a little fenced-in dirt area on the sunny side of our house. We placed a few small boards and logs to protect them from the wind and made their playpen warm and cozy.

As the chicks grew bigger, they needed more food and made more of a mess. Every day we had to look farther to find stinging nettles for their food. During the last two war years, the constant danger of fighter planes was always on our minds. Polli and I tried not to let it bother us. But when we were outdoors, we knew there was a greater danger of an air attack by fighter planes, and we followed Mother's rules to hide right away.

One time, while looking for greens at the railroad freight yard, a fighter plane suddenly appeared shooting at the nearby train station. Shocked and afraid we threw ourselves down on the ground and hid under an empty freight car. When the attack was over, we realized, we were lying in a patch of the juiciest stinging nettles. We felt relieved not to be discovered by the pilot, although our skin was red and itched for hours.

The chickens grew ever bigger and the pen became yet dirtier and more unpleasant to clean. We couldn't wait till our chicks were big enough to freely roam around in the nearby old cemetery, because we had no fenced-in yard for them.

We gave each chick a name. The biggest chicks were always the young roosters. We knew they would soon become a roast chicken for Easter or for one of the other many religious holidays in Bavaria. After several months our chickens were old enough to sleep in the chicken coop, together with the few old, laying hens. Finally, we were happy to be relieved of our burden and our responsibilities.

Early summer 1944, Mother decided not to kill all the young roosters for food. She kept one of them alive. "He'll keep the hens company and happy hens lay more eggs," she explained to us. The rooster was a strong, beautiful young male with golden-brown and black feathers. One day, Polli put the young rooster on a leash and walked him around the house like a dog. However, this rooster didn't behave like a dog. He became very wild, running around in circles to escape from his leash. With a deep red face and an even redder comb he attacked us twins. Frightened, Polli let go of the leash, and the rooster flew up on the next apple tree climbing higher and higher, getting the leash twisted among the branches. Up there on the tree the poor rooster couldn't move or fly away from his unpleasant spot.

When Mother came home she had to climb up a ladder to free the rooster and was attacked by the frightened bird.

Since that day, our rooster behaved like a fiery watchdog, attacking neighbors, friends and the mailman. After a few weeks of this unwanted protection, the rooster ended up in the roasting pan like all his brothers.

Some of our female chicks were not raised for their meat; they grew up to become laying hens. Now, Polli and I got the job of collecting the eggs every day, and we made it a game, playing detectives on a treasure hunt. Some hens laid their eggs neatly in the provided nests in the chicken coop and proudly announced their great deed with a loud cackle; but others were independent and unruly. Three of these hens looked for a softer, more satisfying place to lay their treasured eggs.

Lily, our only white hen, preferred to fly through the upper tilted window into Tante Marie's bedroom and laid her eggs on the pillows. We discovered her hiding place right away, because Lily left dark, dirty tracks on the windowsill, on the glass and all over the floor and bed. After the window was closed, clever Lily looked for a better hiding place for her eggs, and two days later we found her eggs in a neighbor's warm manure heap. "I guess chickens can't smell very well. They don't mind such a stinky place," I thought.

Blondy, our yellow hen hid her eggs in the soft ground under the biggest juniper bush in the old cemetery. Blondy wanted to keep her eggs and attacked us twins. We decided to fetch her eggs by crawling under the big bush together. While the poor hen fought off one of us, the other took the eggs and quickly put them into our collecting bag.

Nuty was a stupid brown hen. She made it easy for us detectives by laying her eggs in our little sister's sandbox and announced it afterwards with her loud cackle. A treasure hunt made so easy was no fun for us detective-playing girls.

One day, while looking for greens to feed our bunny rabbits,-our other responsibility-we found three of our hens dead on the far side of the cemetery. Horrified, we carried the limp bodies of our three hens to our house, determined to find out who killed our beloved Lily, Blondy and Nuty. We asked ourselves, who could have done such a terrible thing? A fox could not have done it. He can't fly and would have to climb over the cemetery walls. A hungry thief would have taken them home for a feast during these meager war years. Polli and I were without a clue and went home to ask Mother.

"Roosters, like deer and many other animals, have their staked-out territories which they protect fiercely. Our three hens probably went too far to the other side of the cemetery. I guess Mr. Veitengruber's big rooster just did what was natural for him; he defended and protected his territory." There was a long pause after Mother's explanation and she stared sadly out the window. We hated when our Mother was sad. To break the silence, Polli asked, "Are you sad Mami because people don't stay in their territories? Is that why we have a war? Mami, are we defending our territory in this war?"

"No," our Mother answered. "We Germans are like the three dumb chickens. We went too far into our neighbor's territory."

15

Christmas 1944

Everything was different from the Christmas the year before. We still lived in the same small town of Solnhofen. Yet so much had changed in our lives, the people we lived with, the town, and the whole country.

The war had struck at our family and friends. We twins were nine year old and already had experienced many hardships. We had lost our father on the Russian front nine months before. Many of our classmates had died during an Allied air raid on the neighboring train station in Treuchtlingen, when several trains with refugees and soldiers were bombed during noon hours. Hundreds of people died in that attack. Among these, many had sought shelter in the passenger underpass and suffocated after both exits had been blocked by concrete pieces and rubble from the collapsed train station.

"Can you imagine, Polli, how awful it must be to be buried alive in an underpass tunnel and slowly suffocate?"

"No, I really can't. I can't believe our friends and all the others who were sitting next to us in class are dead now. We were lucky Mother didn't let us go on the school trip to Treuchtlingen that day."

"Polli, do you know, we would be dead, just like all the others in that underpass? I heard Mother say, 'they haven't even dug out all the bodies from the tunnel yet'".

"I know, Hertha, that's why there was no burial for our classmates, only a general memorial. Rose's mother is still crying whenever she sees me. I feel so sorry for her. It's all so awful, and I don't want to talk about this tragedy anymore. We have Christmas Eve, and I hope we'll get some really nice presents tonight."

"Polli, do you remember when we looked for a Christmas tree with Vati (Father), who was on a furlough from the war last year? At that time nobody knew it was his last. Maybe he guessed it. He was so sad when alone, and drank his homemade liqueur, made from the vodka he brought from the Ukraine. When with us, Vati pretended to be happy, but we knew, he was different."

"Yes, how couldn't I remember, seeing him in such a sad mood? Last year on Christmas Eve, we walked with Vati through a white winter wonderland while looking for the perfect tree to cut for Christmas. We wanted it to be the prettiest Christmas tree we ever had, but we couldn't find one in our grandmother's woods. You remember the large stand of tall fir trees, Vati cleared three years ago? Since then, no firs had grown tall enough to be used as Christmas trees. Later we looked in the state forest for the perfect tree, but couldn't find any nice ones either. Most fir trees were either crooked, or too tall. Vati laughed and said, 'We are so late that most perfect trees are already taken and probably are beautifully decorated in other people's living-rooms.' Unsuccessful in finding the right tree, we stomped through the ankle-deep snow for hours until it was getting dark. I also remember when you asked in desperation, 'But Vati, it is Christmas Eve, and we need a tree today.'"

"Don't worry, my little Polli. We will get one. Look around! Enjoy the pretty snow. Can you see the glittering ice crystals on the frozen trees? Who knows when we'll see another beautiful day like this one again?" Vati tried to sound cheerful while in deep thoughts. Suddenly, I also saw the fairytale winter scene all around us. The reflection of the pink and violet winter sunset on the snow turned its crystals into sparkling diamonds, gleaming against the dark purple sky. At the edge of the snow-covered field stood a row of fir trees like sentinels. But they were all too tall to be our Christmas tree.

"Look, Vati and Polli, it's almost like the trees are already decorated for Christmas with the snow sparkling on their branches!" I called out enthusiastically.

After three hours of unsuccessfully searching for the right Christmas tree, we turned toward town. Meanwhile, the surroundings were completely dark and only the evening star shone brightly to show us the way. Disappointed and cold, we returned to the town through deep snow.

"But Vati, it is Christmas Eve, and we can't go home without a tree," Polli cried. Finally, at the town's Christmas market Vati bought the last tree, a thin and very crooked one. But we did have a tree after all, and Polli, and I were glad for the rare occasion to spend some time alone with our father.

Today, on Christmas Eve 1944 everything was changed. Christmas was not white, but drab and the sky overcast. Polli and I skidded over the hard, frozen ground in our too-tight boots. Hurting with every step, we followed Tante (Aunt) Erna looking for a tree we could cut in the state forest. It had to be fresh if the tree was to be decorated with wax candles; otherwise, the risk of the tree catching fire was too great. Mother had made these Christmas candles using the last emergency candles from this year's supply.

"But isn't it forbidden to cut a tree here?" we twins anxiously asked, worrying about getting caught. Tante Erna only shrugged her shoulder, "Don't worry you two; rather help me find one. This government took so much from us civilians these last years, I think we can take one little tree from the state forest." Tante Erna was not our real aunt; she was one of the nine refugees, now living in our house. At the time, millions of refugees flooded the western parts of Germany. Every house owner in Solnhofen had to provide rooms for several refugees, the number depending on the size of the house and the number of people already living there. Three refugee families moved into our house in March 1944. They were only women and children; because all the boys and men from age 16 to 70 had been drafted into the "Volkssturm" (People's Army) during the final fourteen months of the war.

In previous years, Christmas presents were delivered by the *Christkindl* (Christ child in the form of an angel) on Christmas Eve, while we kids went to church early in the evening. During our absence, Mother performed the role of the Christkindl, decorating the tree and placing the presents under it. In 1944, no more Christkindl came on Christmas Eve. Instead, a live Santa Claus, looking very much like Tante Erna, brought gifts in a laundry basket. Also, the years before, our family celebrated the holidays together with only Grandmother and her sister Tante Marie. This year, we spent Christmas with three additional refugee families and their relatives, crowded together in Mother's living room. This made Christmas Eve very different from the ones we had celebrated before in the small circle of our family.

Santa Claus handed out the presents, reaching into the laundry basket. The presents were wrapped in newspaper. There were names written and little figures drawn on the newspaper wrappings with colored crayons. The presents weren't lavish, and many were hand-made by the women in the house; there wasn't much one could buy that year. Polli and I didn't believe in the Christkindl or Santa Claus anymore, we knew better now and understood the changes that the long war had brought about. At that Christmas in 1944, everybody was thankful to be alive and satisfied for the little there was to give or receive as presents.

Polli and I each received a knitted sweater that Mami had made from wool of one of Vati's former sweaters. Other presents consisted of "*parzipan*" (a kind of marzipan made from potatoes) and *Hutzelmaennchen,* made from pinecones and nuts. Santa Claus played on Mother's piano Christmas songs from East Prussia, we had never heard before. The women were sipping hot, spiced cider, and the refugees were telling stories of their "good old times back home" and of the horror they experienced on their flight from the Russian armies.

Our refugees came from Memel, a city far north in the Baltic area. Their daily lives in East Prussia were so different from the way of life we knew in Bavaria. We twins found it amusing to listen to their strange dialect and thought their food tasted odd. These three families had lost everything, fleeing from the fast-advancing Russian soldiers.

The Kalisch family told us, "We knew early in January that the Russians were coming to East Prussia and packed a lot of our valuable things. We then shipped them to friends in Kiel. However, they were bombed out later and everything was gone. Then we were forced to leave our guesthouse in Memel and took only what we could carry on the last refugee ship out."

The Bluemkes, another refugee family in our house, escaped from the advancing Russians, leaving a house in Koenigsberg (now in Russia and called Kaliningrad).

The old Thieses had to leave their farm behind. In tears, they talked of their losses, their hardship and pain on the long escape route to the West. They described their fears and despair when fleeing to avoid falling into the hands of the Russians. They talked about their desperate escape on ships, and later on trains, overflowing with thousands of refugees, all wanting to go west. There they heard of awful horror stories circulating among other refugees who had lived farther east. In a hushed voice, Mrs.

Thies told Mother about the Russian soldiers, mostly ferocious Siberians, who dragged women from their homes, then raped and killed them afterwards together with their children.

Mrs. Kalisch said with tears in her eyes, "These barbaric Russians not only tortured the people who stayed behind, but burned the villages and destroyed every living creature. Large areas were left in ruins when they moved on. Although we children weren't supposed to hear these stories, we caught parts of them and heard similar stories later from the children of other refugee families who weren't as protective as the adults in our house.

After a while, we children couldn't listen to these sad stories of the adults any longer. We wanted to play with the other kids on Christmas Eve, so we slipped into our winter coats and played in an unheated room downstairs. Even our little sister and brother were allowed to come along with us four older kids. The games we played were simple, child-like copies of things we had experienced, like fighter attacks and bombing raids. We simulated the high shrill of a siren by scraping a nail on a tin can. The older kids acted as American bomber pilots, humming the droning sound of the airplane engines and throwing chestnuts at the little ones, simulating bombs.

Twins with Brother and Sister

"It's not fair!" Guenter Kalisch screamed. "Those chestnuts really hurt. I'm seven years already and can do the same as you", throwing chestnuts at us and imitating the sound of the bombers.

"But the explosions you can't do as well as we, bang, boom, boom", Polli responded, demonstrating it loudly by throwing around metal pails.

The younger kids were hiding below the table or crawling on their stomachs beneath the couch. Our games usually went on until one kid got hurt and ran to his or her mother, screaming. Polli and I were the oldest and mostly got blamed for any trouble.

Not having any new games, we made one up using paper and pencil. We called it the battleship game. Two players drew ten ships on the squares of a sheet of paper, hiding their positions from one another. Each one of the two players hid their ships in the squares, marked by the alphabet horizontally and by numbers vertically. Taking turns with one shot, naming a letter and a number, we kept going until one player sank all the ships of the opponent.

There were many other games we older children made up from what was available and stored in the attic. We dressed up in Grandmother's old clothes from the turn of the century, or we played streetcar with our old twin stroller and imitated the overhead electric wires with clotheslines.

During those last years of the war, life was a struggle for everyone. Adults as well as we children had to learn to make do with what little we had, using our ability and imagination. That Christmas of 1944 was a new experience, not only for us children but for everybody living in our house.

Polli and I wished so much to bring back the happy times we had enjoyed with our father the year before. But we knew it would never happen, and life would never be the same again.

16

A Crush on a King

I admired King Ludwig II of Bavaria, sitting up in the attic of our house in Solnhofen. I was only nine years old and completely infatuated by the image of the king in his coronation attire.

Today, many years later I am still intrigued by King Ludwig II. But I, like most Bavarians, have been puzzled by the mysteries surrounding this king and his death, mysteries still unsolved more than a hundred years later.

My twin-sister Polli and I liked to hide in the attic and read every book we could find, even our grandmother's *Gartenlaube,* a women's journal from the turn of the century. We girls wondered why the young ladies of the nineteenth century fainted so often for apparently no reason. These times were *so* different from ours and we had trouble imagining how it must have been for people way back then.

On one of the cold and rainy days in Germany, we were in our favorite place in a corner of the attic. Our grandmother came up to clean out her storage room, a small fenced-in partition of the attic.

"*Hallo* you two! *Hallo*! Children, can you hear me? Where are your ears? *Zwillinge* (twins) where are you? Hertha, Polli, come and give me a hand!" Our grandmother shouted so loudly that we two girls rushed to her as fast as we could.

"Kochmutti (Koch mother) what's wrong? It's so dark in here, I can't see anything," I answered after I got to the unlit storage room, separated from the main attic.

Kochmutti was not our mother; she was our grandmother. Widowed, she got married a second time the year before, to Mr. Koch, the railroad stationmaster in Solnhofen. We called him *Onkel* Koch, not grandfather.

Our grandmother wanted us to call her Kochmutti. She did not like to be named *Großmutter* (grandmother). "I am too young for that," she said laughingly.

"Kochmutti, what are you doing in here?" I wondered after getting adjusted to the darkness in the little storage room.

"These things are my old belongings: Books, photos, household goods and the likes. I have to sort and clean out everything and throw away what I don't need anymore. We have four families living in this house now, not just one. I want to make available some storage space for the new refugees from East Prussia. They are so crammed in only one room per family; they need space to store things. I call this spring-cleaning. It is spring 1945, isn't it? So, now help me carry down all this junk to the street! The garbage truck will come later and take it to the dump."

"But Kochmutti, there are so many pretty things here. Why don't you give them to the refugees? Maybe they can use them, and we would also love to have some things for our playhouse up here. It would be great. Can we pick out something for us?" I suggested and tried hard to convince my grandmother to give in to my wish.

But she shook her head, "Oh no, we don't move junk from one side of the attic to the other. The refugees can pick out what they want when it's out on the street," our stern grandmother replied.

While helping our grandmother, we kept asking questions.

"Why did you get married again, Kochmutti? Aren't you too old for that? What is a marriage like, and do you love him?" Before our grandmother could answer, I quickly asked another question, "How is it living together with a man every day, Kochmutti?"

Our grandmother threw up her hands over her head, shouting, "No more. No more questions from you two. I really don't have the time now. Come tomorrow down to my apartment at the railroad-station, and I'll answer your questions. Now you have to help me clean out this storage place!"

We helped grandmother carry many items down the two flights of stairs. Most things were already packed neatly in boxes. Then we watched her moving bigger items out from the storage room.

"Oh, Kochmutti, this is the most beautiful picture I ever saw. Don't throw this one out." Fascinated, I kept looking at a gold-framed, life-sized painting.

"It's young King Ludwig II of Bavaria after his coronation", Kochmutti said. "It used to hang in the townhall when your grandfather was mayor. Now, with the Nazis in power, nobody cares about a former Bavarian king anymore." Grandmother shoved the big painting out next to the window. We children followed her, sat down on the floor in front of the painting and stared enthralled at the beautiful young man in it.

A tall slender figure with black hair and black leather boots that reached up above his knees, the King stood in front of a golden curtain. He wore a crown on his head, a dark blue frock and a wide, red ribbon diagonally across his chest. A golden chain and medals decorated his uniform and a sword hung down on his left side. He also wore white gloves and tight white pants, but the most spectacular item was a white ermine fur cloak, draped over his shoulders.

King Ludwig II of Bavaria

Polli and I were fascinated by this painting and ran back to our grandmother in the storage room begging her,

"Kochmutti, can we have this picture for awhile? Oh please, let us have it. Please just for a few days. It is so beautiful."

"All right then, but stop begging and whining! You two are a real pest when you want something. But, you have to promise to read this book I'm giving you. You know, nothing is for nothing in this world. You must try hard to understand the gothic script in this old book; it tells you all about this king."

"Yes, Kochmutti, you know we love to read books, we love to find out more about this beautiful King Ludwig. Are there more pictures of him in the book?" Polli asked excitedly.

"Oh yes, there are many pictures in the book, pictures of him, his marvelous castles and many, many new words for you to learn." She handed us an old dusty book with a dry, cracked leather cover and yellowish brown pages. Happily, we ran with our new treasure to the corner of the attic where we had built our playhouse. Sitting on some old pillows covered with a torn blanket, we snuggled up to one another and started leafing through the pages of the old book. Some pages came loose just by turning them.

"Let's be very careful with this old book, or all the pages will come off and we won't know where the beginning and where the end is," Polli interrupted my wild leafing through the book.

"You are right, Polli. I didn't think about that. But every page is numbered and we can both count to 1000. I like to look at all the pictures first, before we start reading."

We looked at the black and white drawings and some political cartoons but couldn't figure out the meaning of most of them. Excited, we started to read aloud, taking turns, pausing and discussing what we had read. This was the way we always liked to read in a book, it was our twin-way. Every few minutes we looked up from our book to our beautiful fairy-tale king. There, right in front of us, hung the gold-framed painting from a beam in the attic ceiling.

We liked Grimm and Andersen fairy-tales. Now, we loved to read about a real king who lived in the last century and was so beautiful. Every day, after we had done our homework and our daily chore of feeding the rabbits, we sneaked up to the attic to continue reading about this fascinating king. We knew, when mother didn't see us, she would not give us more work to do.

The book from grandmother still had the old gothic scripts, a style of writing very much different from anything we had read before. After some time, we both became quite fluent in deciphering the old scripts, and the unknown words we could guess from the long German sentences. The more we read, the more we became fascinated with the old book; it opened up a whole new world for us, the world of "our fairy-tale king", the former King Ludwig II of Bavaria.

We learned he became king at the age of eighteen, when his father Maximilian suddenly died. Ludwig II tried to rule his country like in the Middle Ages, but didn't get along with his government and his ministers in this constitutional monarchy. However, the Bavarian people loved their young king. They liked to see him speed by in his golden carriage, drawn by four white horses. Ludwig was a romantic; he loved beautiful things and adored the music composed by his friend, Richard Wagner.

Some claimed he loved his cousin, Sisi, but most denied the rumor. Sisi had become the wife of Emperor Franz Joseph of Austria. Sisi and Ludwig had been playmates as children. We felt very sorry for the king who couldn't marry the girl he liked so much, his Sisi with the long brown hair.

King Ludwig's love became building castles, each more spectacular and beautiful than the one before. His romantic dreams became reality in the castles of "*Linderhof, Neuschwanstein*" and "*Herren Chiemsee*". We loved to look at the pictures of these marvelous castles and imagined ourselves in them. Astonished, we learned he built the fairy-tale castle "*Neuschwanstein*" after listening to Wagner's operas.

After several days, Polli's enthusiasm over King Ludwig and his world waned. She wanted to see and do other things than read about somebody long dead. Polli went downstairs to play house with Guenter (one of the refugee kids) and his younger sister, Brigitte, while I stayed in the attic in our little corner, continuing to read and sending admiring looks up to my beautiful fairy-tale king.

I couldn't get over his tragic death. He supposedly drowned in Lake Starnberg, just south of Munich, together with his royal house doctor. I had so many questions the book left unanswered. How could he drown if he was so tall and strong, and such a good swimmer? Some of his people suspected he was murdered because he spent so much money on his castles. His big spending angered several powerful members of the Bavarian government, and they spread a rumor that the King had become crazy. However, the Bavarian people didn't believe this rumor, nor that he had drowned himself, as several of his ministers claimed.

Perhaps more than anyone, I didn't want to believe he had committed suicide. Why would a beloved king, who built all these marvelous castles, want to kill himself? Unfortunately, the book never answered my questions. Puzzled over this mystery and the big question, what happens after death, I sat in the attic, mourning the loss of the long-lost king. At nine years of age, I sat there in the attic looking at the painting of the first man I had a crush on, King Ludwig II of Bavaria.

17

Liberation 1945

On one of the rare, sunny days in April, 1945 the American troops came to our town of Solnhofen.

We children wanted to be outside, enjoying the warm spring weather. Instead, we sat together with all the people, living in our house, in a cold, damp and dark cellar, fortified with sandbags on the only outside wall. Our family had used this place as an air raid shelter during the last years. Today we were told to expect the enemy; the American troops were approaching our town.

Huddled together in the musty shelter since early morning, we endure long hours of waiting. Afraid of what might happen to us all, we sit in silence with our mother, grandmother, Aunt Marie, Aunt Paula and the three refugee families from East Prussia. Meanwhile, noon came and nothing happened. No shots, no bombs, no sound disturbed the unusual stillness in our town. What is to come? Everybody is afraid and the fear is spreading from the adults to us children.

Questions as heavy as the air in the shelter are asked by the fearful, shivering adults. What if the SS (Hitler's special elite force) didn't leave the town yesterday and is hiding in the woods nearby? What if some of the fleeing German soldiers came back and plan to defend our town? After a long pause Mother speaks for everyone. "We civilians are tortured enough. We can't take any more fighting; we long for peace. When will it finally come?"

Our barrel-vaulted, small cellar is not only crammed full with frightened people. Stacked up along the sidewalls are boxes of food and the dearest belongings of everyone. Next to them are crates with Tante

Marie's self-brewed beer and wooden boxes with potatoes, carrots and beets, buried in sand to keep fresh.

Electricity has been out since yesterday. Today, early in the morning, the last SS group blew up the only bridge crossing the river Altmuehl to hinder the Americans' advance. The women in our cellar all hope the SS left town and there won't be any fighting in this small town of no strategic importance.

In the murky dark, I hear the murmur of old Mr. Thies and a prayer of his wife. I can't see them, but I know they are sitting on the long wooden benches placed in front of the sacks and boxes, leaving only a narrow path with just enough space to walk by. We children sit wrapped in blankets on top of the sandbox where the beets are buried.

Our strong, resolute mother, who became that way surviving those many years of hardship during the war, makes most of the required decisions now; not only for us, but for all the others in the shelter. Mother is the only one leaving the basement and checking out what's happening outside. Our Mami is brave, and I am so proud to hear her telling the others not to fear and to stop whining.

In the dark, in front of us children on the bench, sits our grandmother who is unusually quiet. Next to her is Tante Marie, once in awhile telling stories of her childhood to make us forget our predicament. Tante Paula, on her right, uses every long pause to tell about her terrible experience in Nuremberg, when her house was bombed out the year before. Polli and I heard these stories several times, but they are news to the refugees. I remembered Tante Marie's story about the coffee beans her father bought at the county market; she had told it to us twins years before.

Mrs. Kalisch moved into our house with her two children, Guenter and Brigitte. The children are younger than we twins but fun to play with. Their grandparents, the old Thieses from Koenigsberg (now Kaliningrad, occupied by Russia after 1945), came along with them. They were among the first refugees from East Prussia, fleeing before the advancing Soviet troops. Their relatives, the Bluemkes and Erna with young Inge, came six months later. The refugees tell harrowing stories about the war, the bombed-out cities they went through, and the atrocities of the Soviet troops they heard from other refugees. They fled as far west as they could, to escape from the Russians and finally came to us in Bavaria.

While waiting in the dark cellar, Mrs. Bluemke told her story of a near escape on a train from Kiel south. She said, "Train schedules were irregular, because there were so many air attacks on the cities and their train stations. Our train, full of refugees, went through the completely bombed out cities of Hamburg, Dresden, and Frankfurt.

It stopped often in the countryside. When fighter attacks occurred, everybody rushed outside and hid under the railroad cars or in the forest nearby. We didn't get anything to eat for two days till we arrived here in Bavaria."

Guenter Kalisch, only one year younger than Polli and I, sits next to us in the sandbox, wrapped in an army blanket that the last fleeing soldiers left behind. We children are so afraid of what is to come. We hug each other to keep warm and hope for some more stories to break up the endless waiting in the cold, dark cellar.

Eighteen-year-old Inge, Mother's newly acquired helper, tells us how she was buried alive for many hours in the air-raid shelter. Her hometown Kiel was destroyed in several air raids of the Allied Forces during the last years. The air raid shelter was filled with frightened women and children when the house got a direct hit and the ceiling caved in. Everybody in the shelter was killed except Inge. She was lucky, the corner above her head remained standing and air from a crack in the wall was able to get in and kept her alive. Inge was trapped under her feather bed and suffered broken bones and a large wound on her lower right leg. She mutters more to herself than to all of us. "I can't believe it. My mother, sitting on my bed in the corner of the shelter was killed like all the others. Why was I the only one who survived?"

After a long silence, I hear Mrs. Bluemke lamenting, "Oh my God, what will happen to us now? We may all die today. Will the Americans have mercy on us? The barbaric Soviets didn't show any to the German civilians when they occupied Eastern Germany."

Suddenly, every adult in the shelter begins to argue, until Grandmother shouts aloud. "The Americans are not so bad! They come to liberate us! I heard it myself on the BBC radio broadcast. Neighbor Huettinger had built a strictly forbidden short-wave radio in secret up in his attic to hear what the enemy is saying. He was lucky the Nazis never searched his house, or he would have landed in a concentration camp like many before him."

Old grandfather Thies, who had been sitting at the end of the opposite bench, finally stammers, "Stop, be quiet. We all want to stay alive. We all want to see the end of this terrible war and the end of the Nazi regime.

police state under Hitler and his cronies."

We all feel relieved when Mother comes calmly back down into the cellar and reports, "Nothing has happened yet. The Amis (short for Americans) may have bypassed our town to continue south on the Jura-Plateau instead of coming down into our valley. Neighbor Huettinger claims they had been up there in the woods where he had seen movement a while ago."

Polli and I are tired of waiting in the dark; we look at each other and quietly sneak out of the cellar, not before we warn Guenter and Brigitte, sitting next to us on the sandbox, to keep quiet or they would be sorry later. None of the adults saw or heard us and, without saying a word, Polli and I tiptoe out and climb quietly up the stairs to the flat rooftop of our house. Here we have a spectacular view up and down the valley and to the hills above. To our right, high up at the edge of the wooded hills, we look for some movement, but see none. Disappointed, we look at each other. We are no longer afraid, but we want to see the Americans arrive. "They come to liberate us," Grandmother said. We children don't quite know what that means, but it must be good according to the reaction of all the adults down in the cellar.

Suddenly, our frightened mother appears and pulls us back into the attic. "What are you doing up here on the roof top? Are you out of your mind? Don't you know it's dangerous to be outside? Now go, hurry down into the basement!"

A moment later artillery shelling starts. The whizzing noise of grenades flying over our house scares us. We hear them explode nearby. Shrapnel must have hit the window above the stairs leading down to the shelter, because sand and plaster from the walls and ceiling rain down on us. We smell the dry dust and the sulfur vapors from the explosions. It is so quiet in the shelter now. Nobody speaks anymore. I can hear my own breath and feel my heart beating so fast. Polli moves closer and puts her arms around me. It is so still, so awfully quiet in this cramped cellar where no one says a word or makes a sound anymore.

Finally, the silence is broken by Mrs. Kalisch. She covers her face and weeps with a sudden, sobbing noise that she can't control. She cries and cries, holding her little Brigitte on her lap who joins her in unison. "I'm sorry, I just can't stop crying, since our end is so near now. We went through so much on our long trek to get here away from the Russians. We always thought, we would be better off in the west, when the Americans come."

"Stop it!" Mother shouts. "It's not over yet. Be brave and don't frighten everybody any more. We are supposed to be *LIBERATED* now, don't you remember?"

Frustrated with the cowardice some of the people show, she walks up again to investigate the situation after the explosions have stopped. We in the cellar wait for a long time in suspense. It seems like an eternity. Finally, we hear Mother come down. She stops before opening the heavy metal door to the shelter. We can see her dark outline against the dim light from the upstairs hallway as she slowly, weighing every word, says "*I think it's over*, there is no more fighting. I couldn't see much damage in town from our upstairs window. I saw no American troops either. But, I saw a white flag, a bed sheet, in the mayor's window. I think it means the town has surrendered."

Relieved, we all breathe freely again. Someone asks, "Did you hang out a sheet from our house too?"

"No," Mother snaps back, "There may still be SS soldiers hiding in town, and if they see a white sheet hanging out of one of our windows, they could call us deserters and shoot us."

Fear creeps back among our group. We all sit in silence again and wait, hoping nothing bad will happen to us.

Minutes later, we hear a loud knocking at the front door; it might be the Americans! Mother, the only one with some English knowledge, goes upstairs to open the door. We in the cellar wait in fear. What will happen now? Nobody speaks, but 'angst' lies heavy on everyone's heart. Long minutes of waiting follow in silence. Time seems endless. We hear voices and footsteps on the first floor.

Finally, Mother comes back down to the shelter, quiet and in deep thought. Mrs. Kalisch inquires anxiously. "What happened?"

Slowly Mother utters, "It was an American soldier. I don't really know what he said. I couldn't understand him. He sounded like he had a cold. Maybe it's his American slang. But my English is really very poor. I think he asked if we have guns hidden in the house. Or maybe he asked for fresh eggs, after seeing our chickens in the backyard. I really don't know for sure what he asked. I just said to everything, no, no, no. Actually, he was such a young soldier and didn't look fearsome or stern, as the SS-lieutenant did the other day, when he came to observe the bridge from our attic.

I was more scared of the German SS lieutenant than now of the young American soldier."

Relieved, everybody starts talking at once. We take our things and slowly climb upstairs to our rooms. "The immediate danger seems to be over." Mother tries to calm us girls while carrying our sleeping, little brother up to his crib. Polli and I have many questions and ask Mother, but she replies, "No, not now. I really don't have time for it." Although it's only four in the afternoon, we feel so tired. But can we sleep with so many unanswered questions?

18

End of Our Childhood

The war was over. But we nine-year old twins were sometimes depressed and concerned, "What will happen now?" We were afraid of the future and hoped Mother would tell us. But Mother had changed these last years. She was always hurrying, working till late at night and often stressed-out with the daily struggle to get food on the table when everything was scarce. Mother had to barter even for some skim milk at the farm village six miles away. She had little time for us twins and our many questions.

Sitting on my bed one evening, I asked Polli "Has Mother stopped loving us, now after we lost Vati last year and everything is more difficult as before? Grandma explained yesterday, 'Your mother loves you, don't worry about it. She is so overworked these days, since it became so difficult to raise a family.' So Polli, tell me, what can we do to help her?" Sad and worried we looked out of our bedroom window to a foggy morning. The world outside was as gloomy as our thoughts.

I remembered the days when Mother still had time to play with us twins. In my mind I saw her sitting at the piano, her chestnut-brown hair shining in the sun. I remembered how we loved to sit next to her singing children's songs. I realized, these were the good days before the war, and before our little sister Bibi and our brother Butz were born. Suddenly Polli interrupted my thoughts,

"We didn't need them! Everything was just right before they came".

"That's what I was thinking for myself, just now!" I called out. "Polli, do you remember when Mami wore her beautiful blue dress with the big corn flowers? She looked so pretty, and happy."

"Yeah, and she had time to read stories to us and hug us when we came home from Kindergarten. Do you remember when she sang '*Die Bluemelein sie schlafen*' ('The Flowers they Sleep') I hope some time my voice will be as beautiful as hers, and I will learn to play the piano as well as she does."

While we were remembering the good times past, Mother came into our bedroom, dressed in rain gear. A black rubber cape covered her slender figure. Her face looked so sad, we both jumped out of our beds and ran towards her "What's wrong? What happened?" I asked, and Polli repeated the questions almost at the same time.

"I have to talk to you. You are big girls now, and you have to help me. I depend on you, on both of you for some time to come. I know it is a lot what I ask of you girls. But I can't do it alone any longer."

We walked to the kitchen together and sat down at the table. Mother threw a warm blanket over our shivering shoulders and gave us a list of what she wanted us to do during the day. Most of it was nothing new: "Warm the soup for lunch, clean all the dishes in the sink, polish the shoes for everyone and do all the other additional daily duties you are used to do already."

"Fine Mami, we can do it, but why do you look so sad?" I asked, worried about unexpected bad news to come.

"Today and every Sunday, I will have to ride the old bicycle to several farm villages, where I have to trade some of our linens and other articles for food. So now I have to rely on both of you to fill in for me and do what has to be done at home every Sunday. I will be gone most of the day. You will have to take care of your little sister and brother. You also have to prepare the food for dinner. The sauerkraut and the potatoes are cooked. You only have to start the stove and warm the food for dinner. Be careful with the kindling when you start the fire. Let's hope I'll be successful and we can have milk tonight, maybe even butter or pork lard for cooking." Listening intently, Polli and I were beginning to understand why Mother looked so tired and sorrowful. On her way out the kitchen door Mother turned around and added, "If something unforeseen should come up, you can bring little Bibi and Butz to Mrs. Huettinger for an hour or two."

With a deep sigh, Mother padded us on the shoulders and left the house quickly. Left alone in the unheated kitchen I wondered, "Polli, can we do it all? What if something bad should happen?" We looked at each other with determined smiles. We knew we would do our best to please

Mother. Resolutely, we left the kitchen, got dressed, and started doing the chores on the list. Polli began to clean the shoes first. It was an ugly job with the baked-on mud on each shoe. I went down into the foggy vegetable garden to pick some carrots and greens to perk up the watery soup.

When Bibi and Butz awoke, they called for Mother. When they heard she left and we twins were to take care of them, they cried and screamed, "Mami, Mami. We want our Mami!" "Hush now, I promise you, we'll take a walk when the rain stops." I calmed them down and helped them get dressed. I gave each a slice of the heavy dark rye bread and put some homemade jam on it. Starting the fire in the kitchen stove was a problem, even with the wrinkled up newspaper and the dry pine cones, but I managed after a while and felt proud about it.

Later, I prepared some milk from our ration of a Care Package. The powdered milk was lumpy and didn't dissolve in the water, even after stirring it for a long time. Distraught over my unsuccessful effort, I remembered Mother's remark, "Powdered-milk is the only thing our family got from Care Packages. Before these packages reach our town the good stuff disappears on the way. People in dire need loose their scruples, and they steal what they can. Sometimes these items turn up on the black market, but we can't afford to pay the high prices there."

After church, Mrs. Kalisch next door offered to watch Bibi and Butz to let them play with her children. One hour later while we were doing our chores, our little sister and brother came back screaming as loud as they could. At first, I couldn't make out what the noise was all about and worried they were hurt. I felt relieved however, when I heard Bibi complain with a hoarse voice, "Brigitte Kalisch hit me. She is so mean. She hit us both and old Mrs. Thies came to help her, not us. She took Brigitte in her arms and said, 'My darling, my poor '*Marielche*', did these two kids start a fight with you once again'. Mrs. Thies is an ugly old witch with only two teeth, and she talks so strangely."

I tried to calm my little sister and brother, playing with their favorite toys on the kitchen floor and explained, "Mrs. Thies isn't a witch. She and the Kalisch family came from East Prussia, from far away, and people talk differently there than we do."

At that time Polli called from the garden, "Hertha, Hertha, come down quickly, Mrs. Stoeckel has something important to tell us. She heard there are some railroad cars loaded with surplus food from the military left in the Esslinger Tunnel. She said we may come along with her to get some of it." When I came back into the kitchen a few minutes later, my four-year old little brother sat on top of the counter with both hands in the pot of sauerkraut. Terrified, I thought, what shall we do? We can't leave those two little ones alone, not even for a minute. Polli came into the kitchen with an arm full of shoes and hastened to say all-excited, "I asked Mrs. Huettinger. She will take Bibi and Butz so we both can go. Mrs. Stoeckel is so nice, to ask us to come along with her. She says there are several boxcars and wagons full with food and other items left from the war. Everybody can go and get as much as one can carry. She told me to hurry if we want to come along."

Surprised over this exciting news I wondered, "Polli, can we leave the house alone? We can't carry much and it's a long walk to the tunnel."

"Oh you, you '*Feigling*' (coward), you always see problems. We take our crying sister and brother to Mrs. Huettinger and then we fetch our little wooden hand-wagon and run to catch up with Mrs. Stoeckel.

Mrs. Stoeckel knew everything what was going on in town. How did she ever find out about the tunnel? Mother didn't know, or she certainly wouldn't have left in the morning. I hoped we could get some of the canned food, so Mother wouldn't have to trade with the farmers until some later time.

Polli and I tried to keep up with the wide strides Mrs. Stoeckel took. She didn't speak much and sometimes helped us pulling our little wagon. Later, while lagging behind, I watched Mrs. Stoeckel and Polli. They looked funny. There was tall, haggard-looking Mrs. Stoeckel next to my sister, her blond braids bouncing up and down with every step. Polli's face was flushed, she was so eager to keep up with the gait of the neighbor woman. Mrs. Stoeckel carried a tall wicker basket, called a '*Kretzen*,' on her back. It was the same one she used to carry hay home for her two goats. Sometimes, she gave Mother goat milk for Bibi and Butz. I hated goat-milk. It tasted and smelled so strongly. I preferred the blue watery '*Magermilch*' (nonfat milk).

Forty minutes later we arrived at the tunnel and saw many people carrying big rolls of leather and cases of canned food. Everybody took whatever he or she could carry out from the wagons. Watching from the distance I wondered, why do they carry away so many cartons and big rolls of leather? Do they plan to trade it in for food at the black market?

"Look at those hoarders! Just look at them. They can't get enough. I hope they left some for us," Mrs. Stoeckel shouted, hurrying us forward.

The next minute, she disappeared into the tunnel with Polli right after her. I stayed with the little wooden cart on the railroad bridge in front of the big black hole of the tunnel entrance. I couldn't see the end of the tunnel and thought, there must be a curve in it. Actually, I couldn't see anybody or anything in there from my place outside in the sunshine. After a while, I wondered, what if a train comes now with Polli and all these people being in the tunnel. Will I be safe here on the narrow railroad bridge? Then I remembered, I hadn't seen any trains pass by our town since the war ended. Relieved, I was happy again and didn't mind being left behind. While waiting, I enjoyed the warm sunshine and looked down from the bridge to the slow-flowing Altmuehl River. Directly below, I saw the tall reed patches and the shallow spot where we used to go skinny-dipping with Aunt Marie. Yeah, I thought, those were the happy days. I waited and wondered, what took Mrs. Stoeckel and Polli so long? At that time most of the other people had left the tunnel. I became afraid and hoped they didn't get hurt. Shall I go in and look for them? I didn't know what to do. The waiting felt endless. Finally I saw them coming out of the big black hole. Both were carrying heavy things. I hurried towards them. My little wagon, jumping over the railroad treads, made funny noises. Excited, Polli tried to tell me what happened, but Mrs. Stoeckel started already walking home, calling back to load our wagon and hurry.

On the way home, Polli told me what happened in the tunnel. "You can be glad you didn't go in there. Up and down we climbed from one car to the next. Most of them were empty. Toward the end of the train, we finally found two big rolls of thick leather and some green uniforms, but no more food cans. They had all been taken by the people who came before us. Mrs. Stoeckel helped me all the time. She helped me climb up the high steps of the wagons and she helped carry the heavy rolls of leather. Mrs. Stoeckel even gave me two of the uniforms. Ever since Father died she is so nice to Mother and us four children."

We returned home, tired and hungry. It was getting dark and we started the fire in the black iron stove with pinecones, paper and some twigs of dry wood. I opened the pot with the still-cold sauerkraut. Ah, it smelled delicious, and I was so hungry! My empty stomach had been hurting for hours. Polli and I looked at each other and nodded our heads. One spoon wouldn't hurt; it wouldn't even show. When we couldn't resist any longer, we ate one spoon of '*Kraut*,' then another, a third, a fourth and so on. After a few minutes we realized what we had done. Shocked we looked into the pot and saw how little was left of the sauerkraut. We added apple slices to make it look more, but the damage was done and we couldn't find more cabbage in the cellar's big barrel of homemade sauerkraut. With a bad conscience Polli left to fetch Bibi and Butz at Huettinger's and I did some more of our chores on the list.

Finally, Mother came home past eight o'clock in the evening. She looked so exhausted, and barely could lift her legs to climb the stairs leading up to the second floor. We children ran out to greet her. Polli and I helped her carry some of the waxed paper boxes upstairs. "You have been lucky!" we shouted. Mother only nodded and smiled.

"Mami, we have been lucky too." Excitedly, Polli told her about our adventure with Mrs. Stoeckel. Happy and satisfied with our success at the tunnel, we carried our new treasures up to the kitchen for show and tell.

"Stop talking all at once," Mother shouted to make us listen. "Let's first eat the sauerkraut. I am so hungry, I didn't eat all day." Polli and I looked at each other with a bad conscience and said, "We are not hungry. You three can eat it all."

Mother looked at us twins, then looked into the pot with the sauerkraut and remarked with a knowing smile on her face, "All right, I see you two had your share already. But first I'll show you what I got. Look! Eight pounds of pork lard in these wax-containers. We'll add some of it to the sauerkraut; it will make it taste so much better. Instead of meat we'll have pork lard in it and add some potatoes to stretch our meal."

Proud over her successful day, Mother led us to the counter and opened the first wax-box. She took out two tablespoons of the pork fat. Suddenly she stopped, looked in it again, not believing her eyes. Mother opened the next and all the other boxes and, with a red face, cried out in anger, "This mean devil of a man, this hoodlum of a cheating farmer. He told me, 'it is pork lard.' Now I see it's only beef tallow. I'll never trust any farmer again!"

In deep anguish, Mother collapsed at the nearest chair and cried quietly. Polli and I felt so sorry for her. We came and sat next to her with tears in our eyes, "Don't cry Mami. We will help you." I said, giving her a kiss, and Polli added, "We'll always help you. We love you, Mami!"

Our little sister and brother came over and joined us in our crying serenade. Mother had to smile and put her arms around us four children and hugged us tenderly. With tears running down her cheeks and a choking voice she said, "I know. I love you too. You are the best I have in the whole world."

19

Life after World War II

The poet Rainer Maria Rilke wrote, "Don't look for answers. Love the questions and perhaps you will live your way into the answers."

There were no answers after the war for most Germans, having to live in their destroyed cities and devastated country. The future looked dim and uncertain for most Germans. People tried to survive on the bare minimum and sometimes even that was not available. Most tried to make the best of what was possible on a day-by-day basis, except for a few, who used the dire circumstances of others for their own advantage. These were the people who sold things on the black market for outrageously high prices.

Life was as difficult in our little town of Solnhofen as in thousands of other places in the country. The population in Germany had increased during the last war years and right after the war. Well over ten million refugees from the former eastern parts of Germany had to leave their homes and came west. Many had left the rubble of their bombed-out cities and moved to the countryside in the west, trying to socialize among their own circle of people with the same backgrounds.

We children noticed the many changes in our house and in our town but often didn't know the reasons or the circumstances behind what we saw. We were curious and asked questions, but often our mother was too busy to answer or had other excuses, if she didn't like our inquiries.

Memories of that time are still vivid in my mind. Not long after Germany's capitulation on May 8th, 1945, we twins went with our mother to her friend, Frieda Kurt. She lived in a big house they called the Waldschloss, a four-mile walk through dense fir forest above our valley. On our way, we came to the place where the U.S. forces had bivouacked in April. Strewn around the trees were lots of empty ammunition shells, open food cans and weathered old newspapers. Although shocked about the mess left in the beautiful forest, we still looked around to see if we could find anything of use to us.

"There had been others before us searching through this dump," our mother concluded after awhile and dragged us girls away from some garish, colored cartoon pages. We had never seen any comic strips before and stared, fascinated, at the yellow, wilted magazine pages.

"These are no pictures for you. They are garish and strange. I can't imagine why American soldiers would look at stuff like that."

While she pulled us away, curious Polli picked up something, asking, "What's this little thing stuck to the rim of the empty can?"

"Let's see," Mother said, inspecting it carefully. "Never saw anything like it. Guess it's a primitive can opener."

"Look Mami, there is another one still tied on the unopened can. Shall we try to open it?" Polli asked, lifting a small can with the writing SPAM on it. What's SPAM? We didn't know. Eager to find out, we tried to open it. After some experimenting it worked, and to our happy surprise we found ground ham in it, not yet spoiled.

"But Mami, why are the Amis so sloppy and wasteful? Why do they throw away good food? Last week Amis threw grenades into the river, killing many of the fish. Mami, why do they do these things? We would love to eat fish from the Altmuehl, if we were allowed to fish them. Now most are dead and wasted." Mother had no answer, just kept pulling us girls uphill on the gravel path.

Frieda, Mother's friend, greeted us at the door with her daughter, Christa, only one year younger than we were. The girl took us by the hand to show us the toys in her room. Polli and I admired all her gorgeous things displayed on the dresser, but most of all we liked a beautiful toy baby carriage with an old-fashioned porcelain doll in it. The doll could blink, turn her blue eyes and had long curly, blond hair. We had never seen anything so beautiful before and envied Christa for having a father who could get all these toys for her. I wished our father were not dead somewhere in Russia. I looked at Polli and whispered to her turning away and holding my hand over my mouth, "If our father was still alive, he probably would also give us beautiful presents like these."

The only doll carriage we had ever seen before was a white-painted wooden one with small wooden disks as wheels. It belonged to Hilde, a neighbor girl. Her doll was made from knitted stockings and had a simple, painted head.

In the dining room was a coffee table set with beautiful china, holding a gooseberry cake with lots of whipped cream on top. For us hungry twins this was another dream come true, because we never had cream or butter in our house. We could hardly wait till we were allowed to sit down and eat.

Christa turned to us twins and said braggingly, while blinking her eyes, "My father gets these things at the black market, or at the farmers."

On the way home our mother explained to us why some people are better situated than we are, and others are worse.

"You see, the refugees have nothing to trade for food or toys. They came with only the little they could carry. The Kalisches were lucky; they came early in 1944 and could bring some of their belongings with them. But the Bluemkes and many others have nothing. We are actually quite well off. We can live in Oma's house, have a vegetable garden, eggs from our chickens and meat on holidays from our rabbits. We have our furniture and Oma's dishes and utensils. Some refugees have to use homemade cupboards, chairs and other hand-me-downs from neighbors. Some people are so ingenious in their dire need of things, they make their own strainers, pots and pitchers from soldiers' *'Stahlhelme'* (steel helmets) and many other things from former military supplies."

Life after World War II-1

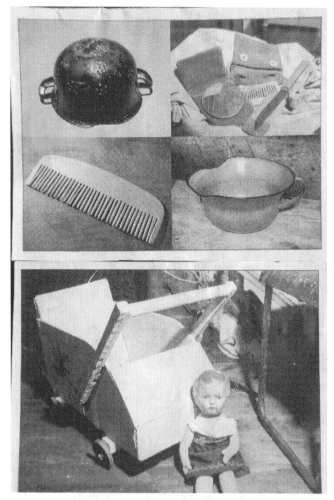

Life after World War II-2

In these difficult years following the war, our Mother was busy all day long preparing food from the little we had. We planted our own vegetables, because the shops didn't carry any, and farmer's markets didn't exist. We had carrots, red and white radishes, leaf lettuce, Brussels sprouts and curly, white and red cabbage in our garden. Dandelion and stinging nettles, collected in the fields, provided for salads. Lacking butter, margarine or any other spread, we toasted the moist, dark rye bread on the top of the iron stove. In springtime, Polli and I snipped off the fresh sprouts on the tips of fir branches and collected them in our wicker baskets. Mother made well-tasting yellow jelly from these sprouts, cooked with our own home-made beet sugar. We kids loved the fir taste of the jelly. It reminded us of Christmas, when the living room smelled like the fir forest from a freshly cut tree.

Tante Marie, living downstairs, had an old fashioned spinning wheel and showed us girls the process of making wool yarn.

First, we helped her wash the dirty, greasy and smelly sheep fleece she got from a farmer for helping him with the harvest. We hung the wet pieces on a clothesline in the attic to dry. Later, Tante Marie took small balls of the dry fleece and pulled them apart into long wads. Then she twirled the wads to thin strands between thumb and index finger. Finally she fed the strands into the spinning wheel, where they were spun into yarn. The yarn got washed and spooled on a two-by-two-foot wooden stretcher to dry. Polli and I learned from Tante Marie how to knit our own scarves, stockings and sweaters. We wore these homemade wool items, which were very warm, but smelly and itchy. We never liked to go to school wearing those items. We thought we smelled like sheep and rather sat shivering in the unheated classrooms.

I remember the hour-long waiting lines forming in front of the grocery stores when CARE packages or other special food items were delivered to Solnhofen. Most of the time, the shelves in the stores were empty, except for potatoes or other food left over from the year before, things no one needed nor wanted.

Often Polli and I stood in long waiting lines in the summer heat and waited for our family's ration of some fish or other rare food items. Mother sent us ahead to wait in line and then joined us just before the store opened. Waiting for a long time was a hard test for ten-year-old girls. Sometimes we played little guessing games, like picking out certain women in the long line, like who was the prettiest or who the saddest-looking. While waiting, we also overheard the latest news of the town.

One time around Easter, our Mother sat at the piano playing her favorite arias from operas. Suddenly we heard a beautiful tenor voice singing from the street below, "*Celeste Aida*" from Verdi's opera. We all ran to the window to see who this Caruso was. It turned out he was an opera singer from Cologne, visiting friends.

During those early years after the war there were no movies shown, the movie theaters were closed. Other luxuries like dancing, shows or concerts which make life pleasant and entertaining were not performed. Reading books and chatting with friends were the only breaks people got from a day filled with work. After they had read the books in the small town library, they borrowed books from friends.

20

Christmas 1946

Although the war ended one-and-a-half years ago, everybody was still struggling to survive. Living from day to day had become a hardship. While millions of people started rebuilding the bombed-out cities and were living among ruins, other city dwellers moved to the country with the hope of finding food and a place to live. However, the country folks didn't like another invasion of people coming into their villages and towns. Their homes were already flooded with refugees from the former eastern parts of Germany.

Without the support of her husband, our mother struggled to get food on the table for her four children. Everywhere in the country, the store shelves were empty and the *Reichsmark* was almost worthless. Our mother was fortunate to have some clothes and household items that she could trade with farmers for food. When this supply was gone Mother needed help. With a heavy heart she sent us skinny twin girls on long walks to farm villages to beg for some food or milk.

It is six in the morning after a cold December night. Polly and I hear Mother calling us to get up and dress. This time, we will be heading for the small farm village of Schoenfeld, 3 miles away from Solnhofen. We have to beg farmers for some milk or butter before we can pick up two Christmas-geese at Mrs. Heinleins.

"Now it is your time to warm some cold hearts," Mother said. "Christmas time is almost here, and you proved to be good in this begging business." But Polly and I hate to go out in the freezing cold. Our thick feather beds are so nice and warm. We don't want to get out of bed as yet.

Suddenly Mother turns on the light and explains to us, "I am sorry, you know you have to be there early, before the other people get there. Hop, hop, out of the beds!" she calls while pulling off our warm feather covers.

Polly, the more dutiful and responsible of us twins, jumps out first while I drag on. We walk on tiptoes, carefully avoiding too much contact with the ice-cold floor in the unheated bedroom. We don't look, but we know there are ice-flowers on the windows, and the water in the washbasin is frozen. We skip the morning cleaning procedure and dress as quickly as possible. Our clothes, like everything else in the bedroom, are cold and unpleasant.

Smelling the warm *Lindenblütentee* (Linden-blossom Tea), we run to Mother in the kitchen. We know, every morning she first starts a fire in the big, black iron stove, then hangs our coats close to it and makes the tea using the boiling water in the enamel kettle. It is a meager breakfast, consisting only of tea and two slices of bread with plum jam Mother made last summer.

Dressed in several layers of clothes, we brave the freezing cold outside and start our long walk in the dark, early morning hour. Our boots hurt, but we have no other shoes to wear. We pull down our thick woolen hats that Mother had knitted for us with yarn from an unraveled sweater of Father's.

We have to walk fast to get to Schoenfeld before the other people arrive, and by moving fast we stay warm. We try not to think of all the possible dangers out there in the dark. According to Frau Seger's gossip, ex-prisoners and homeless people from the eastern countries are still running around in the woods. We know our way in the dark, since we have been on this walk several times before.

Today is a special occasion, because we'll bring home two live geese from Frau Heinlein in our rucksacks. Mother has given the farmwoman father's gold watch, so we could have the once-a-year festive Christmas treat.

Now Polly says what I am just thinking, "I hope she'll give us some milk in addition to the geese, maybe even fill up both of our enamel milk cans, so we don't have to go begging to her neighbors."

Polly and I feel proud not to be afraid anymore being out here in the dark alone. Our way leads us along the frozen Altmühl River, across the old stone bridge and into the hamlet of Eßlingen, where last summer we helped a farmer stack up the hay on wooden poles. Leaving the valley, we climb uphill on a shortcut of the road, through a dense forest of tall fir trees. Holding hands we try not to loose the gravel path in the dark and talk to one another about things past to keep from getting scared.

"Do you remember when we were scared by an owl's call and thought it was a ghost? While we ran home through the dark woods, you fell and claimed you were too scared to get up again. You really were a silly kid, Hertha!"

"Yeah, and do you remember last year, about the same time in December, when I fell on the icy, windblown road? The wind had covered the ice with snow."

Sure, you crybaby, you were scared to come home with a hole in your new pants, while I worried about the spilled milk. You spilled almost a whole liter of milk when you fell and we knew Mother needed two cans of milk for the holidays."

"That day was so awful, I'll never forget. Do you remember Polli, the startled face of Frau Heinlein when she saw us again at her door begging for more milk? She is a really nice person and a good-hearted one too. Even with five children of her own and only a small farm, she gives us milk every time we come."

"Yeah," Polly replies in thought, stopping for a moment. "Most of the other farm women, the stingy selfish ones, just show us their false smiles and say, 'Sorry, try your luck next door.' The Ebers are the worst among those *Habgeiers* ('greedy vultures'), who never give us anything."

"Do you think, Polly, the geese will pick at our hair and braids again like they did last year? These poor geese were so unsuspecting and cute, riding in our Rucksacks, not knowing of their near death."

"I think adults are so cruel, they feed the poor geese with potato dumplings just to fatten them for the big holidays. They force the small dumplings down the animals' throats. Hertha, I don't think I will eat any "*Gänsebraten*" (roast goose) on Christmas Day."

"Polly, forget about the strange things people do. I still have to laugh remembering your face changing from surprise to shock when the goose in your "Rucksack" peed, and the warm liquid ran down your back."

"Yeah, it was awful, but I don't want to talk about it. Besides, we better be quiet now and hurry up. We need to get there in time for the milk before all the others do."

As the winter sun rises over the horizon, the landscape becomes wrapped in a pale, grayish light. Our hearts are beating faster, and we feel relieved and warm, although there is no warmth in the sunlight so early on a winter morning. We come to a windblown clearing up on a wide plateau before we finally reach the farm village of Schoenfeld.

Frau Heinlein's kitchen is nice and warm. She offers us two cups of warm milk and something else we have not seen for years: Heavenly-tasting butter cookies. Feeling warm and cozy, we are delighted by her hospitality and friendliness and don't want to go out into the cold again. Today, we don't mind the sour milk smell hanging in the air everywhere in her house. Although Polly and I know we have to leave soon to be home by noon we linger on in the warm kitchen of Frau Heinlein.

Later on the road back, with the live geese in our Rucksack and two liters of milk, we wonder about the little, neatly wrapped package Mrs. Heinlein gave us for Mother. We walk back home, happily singing Christmas songs. Feeling good again, we enjoy the sparkling winter day, the sunshine and the glistening snow on the trees. We admire the tiny chickadees picking some dried berries in the bushes and a graceful hawk flying high in the pale, blue sky.

On Christmas Eve, when the presents are opened, the biggest surprise is Mother's. In Frau Heinlein's little package, she finds father's gold watch returned with a note:

"Dear Mrs. Birkl, your late husband's gold watch is too big a sacrifice for me to accept. Please keep it as a souvenir of happy moments with him and of the good times you had together.

The two geese will brighten the holidays for you and your lovely family. I hope the twins will have a bite. I know they are disgusted with us adults for killing the animals.

Have a Fröhliche Weihnachten und ein Gückliches Neues Jahr (Merry Christmas and a Happy New Year).

Best wishes, Elfriede Heinlein."

21

Dream and Reality

I was drowning, in a dream, at the age of eleven. Shocked, I woke up and started wondering. What does it mean? I wondered even more after the same dream happened several times.

In my recurring dream, I saw myself skipping happily down a grassy hillside on a sunny morning. Suddenly there was a steep cliff in front of me and down below a lake. I couldn't stop in time and fell into the clear water. After the impact, I always saw myself slowly drifting down to the bottom while the air bubbles of my breath were rising up in front of my eyes. At the bottom of the lake it felt so beautiful and peaceful. In my dream, I saw myself lying on the sand with fishes gliding above me through the plants. I no longer felt afraid when I saw no more bubbles rising, and watched the sunlight filtering through the clear water between the dark shadows of the water lilies. In every recurring dream I saw myself lying on the bottom of the lake, thinking, 'so this is what it feels like to be dead'. At that moment, I always woke up.

One year after the first dream, my twin sister and I took swimming lessons to make sure there was no more reason for my recurring dream of drowning. The river Altmuehl with its green water flows slowly through Solnhofen and was the only place where one could swim. In 1947, our small town had no modern swimming pool. Instead we had a *Badeanstalt* (a place for bathing and swimming) in a small, cordoned-off part of the river. There was a row of little wooden cabins, surrounding a grassy square on three sides, at the river's edge. Wooden platforms and walkways had been fastened to four huge steel pontoons that were floating in the river and anchored on the shore. Two different-sized rectangular wooden basins hung from the pontoons into the water. The small one was shallow and meant for little children to splash around in. The large, five foot-deep basin was used by adults who couldn't swim. Our swimming lessons were given in the large basin by an instructor from the gymnastic club. The basin had a slippery wooden floor and a wooden fence all around.

On our first day of lessons, Polli and I stood with fifteen other children in a long line on the wooden walkway, listening to the instructor. Each one of us children had a life preserver, made from big, six by ten inch cork pieces, tightly tied around our waist. We girls felt ashamed in our wet cotton swimsuits, clinging to our bodies, while the boys stood nearby having fun watching, laughing and making naughty comments to one-another.

Finally when time came to start the swimming lessons, Polli and I followed the instructor's directions exactly. The instructor walked, or stood above us on the wooden planks, checking every child and giving orders. After the one-hour lesson, all children were graded for best effort. Only naughty Heinz Opel, the bully, who had always interrupted the lesson, failed the class, and we girls enjoyed watching him being pushed back into the water.

Exhausted and cold after being in the water for an hour, Polli and I walked to a sunny spot on the outside edge of the wooden walkway to warm and dry ourselves. While we bent down to spread out our towels in the sun, Heinz Opel sneaked up behind us and pushed Polli and me into the deep river.

What a shock! Suddenly I found myself in deep, dark green water, trying frantically to get to the surface. However, every time I thought I would succeed, I found myself underneath one of the big steel pontoons. I was running out of air and started to panic. It was an awful and terrifying feeling to be without air, caught below the pontoon. Although exhausted, I kept telling myself, "I can't drown. I can't drown, because in my dream I drowned in clear lake water and not in green, murky river water." Then my thoughts stopped.

When I came to myself again, I saw my sister Polli bending over me, with tears streaming down her cheeks. She had reached the surface right away and was helped out of the river by the instructor. He and several men frantically searched the water for me and found me, unconscious and trapped underneath one of the suspended walkways between two pontoons.

Finally rescued, Polli and I were so happy to be alive and together again. We held each other, tightly wrapped in our towels and a woolen blanket from the instructor. After a long time, still shivering and cold, we promised each other to learn to swim as quickly as possible. We swore to one another to be more watchful, and never ever let any bully try to drown us again.

22

Childhood Memories

In 1947, spring was slow in coming; yet some weeks before it actually arrived we felt an inkling of its impending approach. In some windows in the neighborhood we could see flowerpots with cyclamen, daffodils and tulips in bloom. Sometimes we pressed our noses against the glass and looked at the bright colors, imagining their fragrance.

Eventually, spring did arrive and brought white snowdrops and colorful crocuses in the sunny patches in Mother's garden. In April, tiny violets, with colors from a light-blue to a deep-purple, peeked through short bunches of fresh, green leaves. Daffodils, tulips and irises, our Mother's pride, were admired by everyone walking by. What I remember best of all was the explosion of white, violet, purple and burgundy-red lilacs blooming in May. We children picked armfuls and buried our noses in the heady fragrance of the blossoms, and their powerful aroma filled the air for weeks in the garden and in our living room.

Once a week after school my twin sister Polli and I went into the woods with a little wooden hand cart to collect pine cones. We also looked for dry branches and roots of dead trees, the only firewood one was allowed to collect in the forests. After the war, a family was allotted a meager yearly supply of coal and wood. We children knew the best places to find big, dry pinecones and collected them in burlap sacks that we loaded on our little wagon. After some painful experiences when trying to loosen dry roots with our bare feet, we developed a system by pushing them back and forth with a heavy stone.

Sometimes on a hot summer day, the pleasant aroma of the pine trees tempted us to linger and lean on one of the big tree trunks. Sitting on the soft dry needles and enjoying the smell and the warm sunshine on our faces we didn't care about the stains and spots of sticky resin on our clothes.

On other occasions, we walked up to a patch of big, old beech trees and collected the little triangular seeds we called 'Bucheckerln'. Mother pressed them to retrieve cooking oil, an item not available in the stores at the time. Filling our wicker baskets with the tiny seeds was a tedious job. The fresh, green beech leaves filtered the sun and left us in comfortable cool shade on hot summer days. We liked the earthy, musty smell rising from the layers of dry and rotting leaves on the ground. On our way home, we loved to make 'Purzelbaeume' (rolling over) down the sloping meadows.

One bright sunny day when we sisters were lying on our backs in a meadow full of wild flowers, we looked up to the sky and imagined castles, animals or big monsters in the cloud formations. Drowsy from the humming of the bees around us and the warmth of the sun on our bodies, we were happy and content.

In springtime we had fun collecting the big brown and black 'Maikaefer' (Maybugs). We imprisoned the poor animals in little cardboard boxes with holes. We filled these boxes with fresh leaves to feed the bugs. Our chickens loved to gobble up these bugs after we became bored playing with them. Tante (Aunt) Marie told us the chickens will lay especially big eggs after such a treat and their eggs would taste better than ever.

Summer days were frequently rainy. I recall a rainy day in a dark forest of tall fir trees; the trails through the woods were slippery with soggy needles. Ferns dropped their heavy heads and water droplets ran along the center of their arched branches like on a track. This day, the usually dark forest looked even darker and every sound we heard, we imagined to be from wild animals or escaped German war prisoners, preying on little girls. We had been warned by our mother to beware of bad people, who might kidnap or harm women and children. During the early years after the war, many former prisoners were still roaming the countryside.

One day Polli and I were wading barefoot in a small brook, enjoying the feeling of mud squeezing through our toes, so soft and pleasant compared to the hard crushed lime stones on most of the roads in our town. Shoes were a rare item, and we wore them only to school and to church on Sundays. In the middle of the brook we found a large flat rock, a perfect platform to build a tiny house with the twigs, pebbles and moss we collected. The gurgling water rushed around us, and the cold clear water chilled our bare feet.

Some days we gathered delicate rose petals and put them into little boxes thinking we could preserve their fragrance for the winter days.

In my mind, I experience again the summery smell of fruits when Mother made jams. We liked to help clean the strawberries, raspberries, cherries and plums, and would linger around so we could lick the dishes and bowls afterwards. Mother used homemade, heavy brown sugar, we helped to prepare by peeling, chopping and pressing sugar beets. Afterwards Mother cooked the molasses for many hours till it crystallized and became a heavy, dark brown sugar.

Every other week was laundry day, and we twins had to help after school, because it was a full day of heavy work for Mother. The thick, steamy air in our stone-floored laundry room became so dense, we couldn't see the two windows; and the old water pump with the long handlebar looked like a shadowy witch. The room was filled with big wooden buckets and oval-shaped tin washtubs where the dirty laundry soaked in cold water from the night before. Early in the morning, Mother started the fire under the big kettle with the wood we had gathered in the forest. During the hours that it took for the water to boil, Mother scrubbed the laundry on a washboard. Later the clothes were cooked for two hours in the big kettle, built into a square masonry oven. When we girls came home from school at noon, we helped scrub the dirty laundry for the second load till our fingers became sore. We didn't like that chore, but we enjoyed the steamy soapy smell when the hot wash was transferred with a big wooden pole from the kettle to the tubs for a cold water rinse. A homemade brown slimy liquid soap was the substitute for non-available detergent and soap bars. By the end of the day, Mother was so exhausted, and we children felt sorry we couldn't help her more. Looking back, I am glad we have electric washers and dryers today.

Once a week, everybody took a bath in the laundry room. There was no gas in Solnhofen for heating, electricity was expensive and coal was rationed and limited, so a warm bath was a luxury only enjoyed on Saturdays. At this time, a bed sheet was hung on a clothesline across the room for privacy. There was water for only one warm bath per family and we had four families living in our house. One had to take turns. Polli and I took our baths together in the big oval tin tub right after Mother. Our job afterwards was to wash and scrub our little sister Bibi and brother Butz.

Those two kids, five and three years old, were so dirty, we assumed they rolled in the dirt just before having to take a bath. Usually they screamed as loud as they could when we tried to clean them. When Mother came to find out what caused the racket, they claimed we hurt them. Most of the time, it wasn't true, but we were blamed for it anyway. These situations made us twins hate to be their sitters and caretakers, a job we had to do for many years while Mother was working at the quarry, polishing lime stone tiles. It was the only job available for her at the time. Sometimes Mother was away trying to barter for food at the farmers even on Saturdays.

I recall early winter mornings, when it was still dark, and we crawled out from the comfortable warmth of our feather beds and put on school clothes. We hated the scratchy woolen underwear and the long woolen stockings held up by garters. Our knitted jumper and sweater were made from Tante Marie's homespun sheep fleece. Bundled up in heavy capes made from soldier's coats we went out into the cold and often slushy outdoors, when the day was just beginning to get light. We trudged off reluctantly on our one-mile walk to school, listening to the church bell tolling time every fifteen minutes.

At Christmastime, the smell of cookies being baked and the spices of vanilla, anise, ginger and cinnamon wafted through the house. Excited by the smells and the warmth in our kitchen, we enjoyed sitting next to one another near a window, watching the snow falling outside, covering the frozen vegetable garden. We could hardly wait till Christmas Eve when we finally could eat the cookies and enjoy the one present we twins received together. I remember the smell of the burning homemade wax candles on the Christmas tree, and the warm light they made seemed magical to us twins. Mother played at the piano while we children and all the adults in the house sat next to her and sang Christmas carols.

Contrasting with the lovely aroma of the cookies at Christmas was the look and smell of the large bottle of castor oil, standing on a sideboard in our kitchen. My mother used caster oil as a medicine to treat digestive problems. The bottle had a picture of a fisherman dressed in a yellow slicker, holding a large fish by its tail. One eye of the fish seemed to be glaring angrily at us. Adding to the repulsive picture were thin, dried-on streaks of oil that ran down the sides of the bottle, a constant reminder of the horrid contents inside. With this picture in mind, I can now, so many years later, remember the fishy taste and rancid smell of the cod liver oil.

Polli and I hated to take this medication and felt we deserved a reward afterwards. When none was given, we tiptoed into the living room and helped ourselves to the hidden cookies from the big jar behind a stack of sheet music next to the piano.

Whenever I see, smell or taste similar things today, my childhood experiences come back to mind.

23

School after the War

Polli and I are on our way to school. It is a hot and humid day in June and we drag our feet. Polli and I wish summer vacation were here. "But vacation starts only in August," Polli reminds me. We twins don't like the old Mr. Hoegner who became our teacher after the war.

"He is as old as Methuselah," Mother said. "He used to teach me when I was a child and I didn't like him either. He should be retired long ago, but there are no replacement teachers in our little town. As you know, all the former teachers have to be 'de-nazified' now. It means, in the Hitler regime, they had to join the Nazi party to teach, and now their past has to be examined and cleared to get a new teaching license."

Polli and I like to stomp into the milky puddles left from last night's rain on the crushed limestone road. We have fun splashing one another's shoes and stockings, forgetting all about school. Suddenly we hear the bells on the old church tower ring eight a clock, "School starts now?" we both scream and run as fast as we can. We reach the classroom being out of breath, and our hearts are pumping.

"It's you twins again-always tardy," gray-haired Mr. Hoegner scolds, looking sternly over his rimless glasses. We sneak into our seats behind two little wooden desks next to us. Herr Hoegner continues writing some multiplication tables on the big swivel blackboard in front of the room. He is a small man and stands next to his desk on a raised wooden platform to have a better view of the class room and to look more imposing. The sun shines through the big windows. They are still partly patched up with cardboard from the air-raid years, leaving his body in the shadow and his head brightly illuminated. He squints, pulls up one side of his nose and mouth, giving his face a grotesque look.

Herr Hoegner has all the children repeat the multiplication tables aloud and flips the free-standing blackboard over to its empty side. He orders the class to repeat all the multiplications aloud again. We children are all scared. If we don't remember, we know the usual whipping will follow. Herr Hoegner is always in a bad mood; he doesn't seem to like teaching us children. His cold gray eyes look sternly over his glasses into the classroom, inspecting, suspecting. With a sarcastic expression, he pulls poor Otto by his right ear out of his seat. Otto must have done something wrong. The poor boy stands in front of the old teacher with a bright red face and shakes all over. Herr Hoegner gives him three hard slaps on his palm with the whip and Otto wets his pants out of pain and fear. No one laughs in the classroom, because every student is afraid he will be next.

When the bell rings for the break we all hustle out into the wide-open hall. We look eagerly into our little brown bags to see what sandwich Mother packed this morning. "Again the old stupid rye bread with no butter or margarine, only with the homemade jam already soaked into the bread," Polli protests out loudly. During the rest of our half-hour break all children have to walk in long lines, circling the schoolyard under the strict eyes of a custodian. I don't mind being out in the fresh air after the heat in the steamy classroom.

Herr Hoegner teaches music twice a week. He also plays the organ in our church on Sundays. Although we love singing with Mother at the piano, old Mr. Hoegner spoils all music for us. He walks in front of us children, who march up like soldiers in a parade and stand stiffly in two rows. He plays his violin while we all have to sing folksongs in chorus. If one of the singers doesn't open his mouth as wide as expected, Mr. Hoegner pokes the violin bow into the child's mouth to pry it open. Even songs Polli and I usually like, we don't enjoy in his music class anymore.

Once a week, religion, an official subject of the curriculum, is taught in school by the pastor of our Lutheran church. A priest teaches the few catholic children in town, using a separate room. Today, Polli whispers to me, holding one hand in front of her mouth, "I like Mr. Hilpert. He tells the stories of the bible so beautifully, just as if it happened yesterday."

"Yeah, I remember last time you had tears in your eyes when he described Jesus' death on the cross," I remark, lost in thought.

"What do you mean Hertha? You were crying too and sniffled all the time until he took you in his arms and walked you outside into the hallway to calm you down."

One year later, in 1947, we all rejoiced when we got a new teacher in sixth grade. Mr. Eberle was tall, slender and soft-spoken. He always wore the same faded, brown suit which matched his hair. He was the first young teacher in our town allowed to teach after the war. All children liked Mr. Eberle. School was fun again. Polli and I enjoyed learning again and liked to do our homework promptly every day. We were no longer afraid of making any mistakes like we did with Mr. Hoegner.

One year later, when we took the entrance exam for the lyceum (high school for girls) in Treuchtlingen, I was so afraid of failing the difficult test. I panicked and couldn't think. I became so paralyzed with fear, I flunked the exam. Because I had good grades before and my twin Polli did so well on her test, the principal made an exception and accepted me. I was so happy not to be separated from my sister with whom I had spent almost every day of my life.

24

A Strange World

The first three years after the war were times of rebuilding and adjusting to a new world around us. But these years were also times of continued sacrifice and hardship. They taught us curious youngsters lessons we never forgot. We two skinny and shy eleven year-old girls with a pale complexion and blond ponytails were growing up fast during these years. Polli and I spent many hours talking in bed about our observations and impressions.

"Isn't it strange Polli, that American soldiers love chewing on something they call chewing gum? I don't really know what it is, but I watched them chew on it for a long time and then spit it out. I wonder why they are doing that. It must taste good, I guess. But how come that they chew so long on a single little piece?"

"I don't know Hertha. I wonder why they call the American soldiers, 'GI's'. I can't figure it out. Have you ever heard what it means? And these soldiers seem to have lots of cigarettes because they throw them away only half smoked," Polli wondered crawling into my bed.

"And Polli, I saw German men pick them up and continue smoking them all the way down. Do they need to smoke a cigarette so badly to do that? These days one can get cigarettes only on the black market for a lot of money. I heard Mother say the other day that many women, addicted to smoking, hook up with the American soldiers to get their supply of cigarettes. She and Grandmother agreed it's degrading for German women to run after the Amis. Polli, I know for sure, I will never start smoking cigarettes when I'm grown up."

"Listen to this, Hertha. I heard Mrs. Stoeckel say sadly, almost angrily, 'It's not right for German girls to date American soldiers.' "Why do you think they do it, for the cigarettes, or because so many German men their age died in the war?"

"No, don't you know? It's for the chocolates or the cigarettes, you *dummy*"

"Sure I knew it, Hertha. I wanted you to call me a dummy, so I can call you a dummy next time. Hah, hah, I fooled you this time, didn't I?"

Polli and I loved this game of asking each other questions, knowing that most of the time we would have the same thoughts about our changing world.

One evening, when electricity was turned off, I slipped under Polli's feather cover and whispered to her so Mother wouldn't hear us talking so late.

"Now it's my turn to ask a question first, Hertha. I think it's sad what happens these days when some husbands come home from POW camps in Siberia and find their wives living with another man. You know, whom I mean? I mean Mrs. Bluemke and that much older man that moved in with her; it's shameful, don't you think so? Her husband was drafted into the '*Volkssturm*' only two month before the war was over. He hasn't been declared dead and might still come back.

"Yeah, many women who do this probably thought their husbands were killed in the war because they haven't heard from them for so long. It's so hard for women to survive alone these days. We know, we see Mother's example every day. I wish our father wasn't in Russia dead and would come home like Mr. Huettinger did."

"Oh sentimental Hertha, still hoping the military made a mistake and father will come home again. That would be heavenly, but I don't think it will happen." Polli, knowing all the answers, continued talking about things we observed, now in a hushed voice because we heard footsteps outside our bedroom door.

"I wonder why so many foreigners are begging and walking in our streets. They come from Poland and Hungary I heard Mother say. Why do they come here where there isn't even enough food for us? They must be fleeing from the Russians like our German refugees from East Prussia did." Then Polli added sadly, "These beggars have no home and live in '*Sammellagern*' (refugee camps)."

"I don't know Polli, I heard many of these poor, homeless people will be able to immigrate to America soon. However, all these German '*Kriegerwitwen*' (widows of fallen soldiers) with children and no husbands aren't so lucky. Some days we see strangers, handicapped soldiers in town, who came back from the prison camps. I wonder why don't they get together with the widows and help one-another? Wouldn't that be a solution to their troubles?"

"It's a great idea, Hertha. You always feel sorry and want to help people, but we are kids and nobody will be listening to us. I thought of something I think is funny. With the Marshall Plan money, they give us free school-lunches every day and weigh and check each child once a week to see if we are healthy and gained some weight. I am glad we get the warm cocoa and the soup; but I wonder, do they want to fatten us up like Mother fattened the geese the days before Christmas?"

"Ha, ha, ha, Polly, but did you hear that American people are sending Care Packages with food to prevent us from starving? Who gets these packages? I never saw any of them! We still are hungry most of the time, and Mother can't provide enough food for all of us. I hated the nettle salad and the blank toasted pumpernickel bread she served tonight." I turned around holding my hands to my hurting stomach and asked,

"Polli, did you see this morning that the trains are running again? The wagons are literally stuffed full with people. Like Mother, these people are probably looking to barter for food, going by train now instead of riding a bicycle. I saw people climbing through the windows, because they couldn't get out through the doors. That's how full each car was."

"Yeah Hertha, the trains are a big help for people to get around now. It took a long time after the destruction in the war to have the bombed-out trains and train stations repaired again."

"Polli, you won't guess what I saw yesterday afternoon. Eva, from across the street, went to the dance over at Hotel Adler. She wore a new dress from a CARE package and had painted a line on the back of her legs to make it look like she was wearing nylon stockings. Do you think people wouldn't know?"

"Have you heard Hertha, these new nylons are so expensive. She probably couldn't afford to buy any of them and wanted to impress the young men there."

While we twins were whispering and laughing under our feather covers, we didn't hear our Mother come into our bedroom with a flashlight saying, "It is ten o'clock now, girls, time to stop talking and finally going to sleep. Tomorrow is another day. Stop now or I have to separate you and put one of you in my bedroom." This warning worked immediately. Polli and I felt we couldn't sleep when separated.

Two years later there were no more blackouts in the evenings. We girls were allowed to stay up longer with all the adults of the house who assembled in Mothers heated living room. During those evenings Polli and I loved looking at the beautiful pictures of Mother's art-books, where years before we used to scribble and draw little figures on each empty page. At twelve years of age now, we appreciated the beautiful art pictures.

One evening I heard Mother say to Tante Marie, "Last month, on June 20, 1948 Germany finally got the long awaited '*Waehrungsreform*' (currency reform). I hope it will bring about a huge change in Germany's recovery. But one only gets 10DM (Deutsch Mark) for 100 RM (Reichsmark), and one person can receive no more than a total of 80 Deutsch Mark. This is very little money even with the new low prices. Our whole family can't live on just 400 DM! I have to find additional work outside the house right now. But there are only jobs available in the quarries up on the hills."

Polli and I hoped things will get better after we overheard Tante Marie saying, "This year we are going to get a new government and constitution. Germany will be named the '*Bundesrepublik Deutschland*' (Federal Republic of Germany). This country and the German economy will recover, and new jobs and consumer goods will be available again."

In our beds at night we twins kept wondering, why the store shelves were empty before the currency change and now they were full of goods to buy, but people had no money. It is a strange world after all we twins concluded, turned around and went to sleep.

25

Our First Train Ride

"Hallo Hertha, Polli! Come, quick, I have great news for you!" Mother called us twins, interrupting our play. News is always exciting for twelve year-old girls, especially rare news.

"You've been invited to go to Dolling for a vacation. But you will have to go alone, because I can't get away from work. I know this will be your first trip without me. You'll travel by train and change in Ingolstadt to a smaller train. In Dolling you will meet Onkel Karl and his family and see the place where your father grew up. Isn't that exciting? What do you say?"

"But Mami, how can we go without you? We don't know them and we never traveled on our own," Polli wasn't sure she was happy or sad.

"Sure you can. You are smart kids and you have each other. I know you'll manage just fine. Besides, next to the castle there is a big farm that belongs to Onkel Karl. There is lots of food and you finally can eat as much as you like."

With this encouragement, Polli and I boarded the big steam-powered train several days later. From the open window, we waved to Mother with uneasy hearts. Too nervous to sit down, I reached for Polli's hand and stood by the window watching the lovely Altmuehl river valley with tall limestone rocks bordering it. The valley was covered with patches of forest and fields with wheat and rye. Nestled in between were gray-roofed villages with one or two churches in the middle of each one.

Closer to the city of Ingolstadt the countryside became wide and flat, and we lost interest looking out the window. We were so nervous about changing trains at the big railroad station in Ingolstadt. "How can we find the right train among so many others?" I asked Polli. When we got off the train we tried to read the posted train schedule at the platform, but couldn't make sense of all the confusing numbers and symbols. We stood there worried and puzzled until a farmer came to our rescue.

"Where are you traveling to? Oh, you want to go to Dolling. I see the address on your suitcase. That's where I 'm going. Just follow me. Our little train was waiting far over on the other side of the station. "Hurry, we don't want to miss it."

We helped the farmer carry his cloth-wrapped bundle and ran down and then up a flight of stairs till we came to the last platform. It was exciting to board a real old-fashioned train looking like the one in our picture book. Excitedly, we boarded the little train with the friendly farmer. Not nervous any more, Polli and I enjoyed the much slower ride on this vintage train.

"Look at the tiny locomotive, blowing black smoke, and the cute little carriages!" Polli shouted turning to me. Bothered by the smoke, we closed the window and joined the farmer on the wooden benches. Watching the farmer sitting opposite from us, we saw something moving in his big bundle.

"What do you have in there?" Polli inquired, staring with wide-open eyes at his bulky bundle.

"Oh it's just my goat. You remember the song about the farmer and his goat?" The man looked at us, smiling.

"Oh sure," I replied, "Would you like to hear us sing the song?"

Encouraged by the man's nod, we sang the popular song about a farmer, who tied his goat to the end of a slow-moving train, because no animals were allowed inside. When the farmer wanted to get his goat at the next stop, he found only its head and rope still tied to the caboose.

While singing I watched the farmer's bundle move. The bundle seemed too small for a goat to be in there. "It's not a goat at all. I heard some cackles. You have some chickens in there, don't you?"

Surprised, the farmer laughed, remarking, "You are a clever one, aren't you?" After a while the farmer said with a smile, "So, you are spending some time in Dolling visiting my friend, Karl, in the castle."

"Yeah, he is our uncle; our father Toni grew up there," Polli blurted out. "But how did you know we would visit our uncle Karl?"

"Well, you girls look so much like Toni when he was your age. We went to school together."

Polli and I looked at each other wondering, why he would say that, because people at home would always say we look like our mother. Do we look like our mother or like our father? Glancing at one another, we girls decided we look like ourselves and no one else. We smiled and nodded to one another. Often, we twins didn't need to talk about thoughts, because we had the same thoughts much of the time. Traveling in the farmer's company, we had a great time talking with him and were taken by surprise when the conductor called out, "Next stop Dolling!"

26

Vacation in a Castle

At twelve years of age, life is exciting, especially if you are invited to spend two weeks of vacation with relatives in a castle. Our mother couldn't get away from work and expected us twins to travel alone. Polli and I worried in the beginning of our trip but felt proud after we arrived on our destination in the small farm village of Dolling.

When we arrived at the train station, there was nobody to pick us up. Seeing our worried faces, standing at the platform and looking around, a farmer approached us and asked, "You look lost. Where do you two girls want to go?"

"We expected to be picked up by our uncle, Mr. Foerster. He lives in the castle", Polli answered,

Oh, Mr. Foerster! I know who he is and where he lives, although I have never met him. Don't worry, I'll show you how to get there. Follow me to the end of the village, and a little while farther down the road, you'll see the castle." Relieved, we followed him, expecting to find the new shiny white building we had seen in Mother's old photograph. Eager to meet our relatives, we hurried on our way through the village.

Full of expectations, we turned from the asphalt road into a willow-lined gravel road, leading to a dirty pond filled with shrieking geese and ducks. There, behind more willow trees, we saw a large, gray, three-storied building with a tower on each of the four corners. "Is that the castle?' I asked Polli hesitantly.

"This building looks so different than the one in Mother's picture! Its plaster walls are cracked and dirty, with holes all over." Polli answered with a frown and a minute later she shouted, "We are here, we finally arrived!"

Happily, we ran towards the building, never wondering why we were not picked up at the train station. A minute later, we stormed into a big kitchen on the ground floor, following an enticing smell.

A heavy-set, old woman stood at a window and turned toward us. This must be Grandma Foerster I thought. "Oh, my God, you are here!" She exclaimed. "We didn't know you were coming today. My, my! Let me look at you two. You are so skinny. You surely look like your father's children. Oh, how I miss my poor Toni. He died so young and couldn't see you growing up into two pretty little girls.-Now here I keep talking, and you must be starved."

"We are not little and we are not starved," Polli quipped back.

"Oh sure, you are two big girls and just traveled a long way all by yourselves." Grandma Foerster ignored Polli's rude reply. "Come over and sit down at the table. I will fix you some hash browns with ham and eggs. I'm sure you will like that."

While waiting, we watched this new grandmother, we just met for the first time, getting a heavy iron frying pan and setting it on top of the wood burning stove. Grandma Foerster looked very much like our Oma at home, only older. She had similar features and her hair was also brushed back with a bun at the neck. Sure, I thought, looking at her, I can see now they are cousins.

The large, dark kitchen had only one window, set deep into a three-foot thick wall. There were several shelves on the wall with lots of dishes and cans, boxes, baskets and other kitchen utensils. Some open barrels stood along the wall, filled with butterfat, lard, prunes and other items. Looking at these treasures, I knew, our mother would have loved to have some of these rare items. Grandma Foerster cooked us a delicious lunch and made us feel at ease. With her rough but good-natured way, we girls decided, we like this newly discovered grandmother. After we finished eating, she took us both in her big arms, hugged us and said, "Oh, you poor girls, you come at a time when only Ella and I are home. Your uncle Karl is out in the fields and our 'Fine Lady' is at the equestrian show in Ingolstadt. Your Aunt Ruth likes to show off her new stallion. Sorry, I called her a fine lady because she lives upstairs and never comes down into my kitchen. But she really is a nice person, as you will see."

A while later Ella, our cousin, came into the kitchen. She was a year younger than we, and I was surprised to see her being as tall as we were. I liked Ella's brown eyes and brown hair, but I found her square-shaped face with a pronounced chin, funny.

Ella felt lonely and said, "I 'm glad you came. My sister Freya and my little brother Roland are in Rothenburg with my other grandmother." Coming closer to us she said, "You are really not so bad-looking," inspecting us from head to toe. "I heard you would be half-starved. It must be terrible not having enough food to eat."

Polli interjected, "We are not starved. We just don't have all those good things to eat like you do."

"I didn't mean to hurt you," Ella replied, pushing us out of her grandmother's kitchen. "Would you like to see the castle? Luckily it was not destroyed during the war. Come on, I show you around." She led us upstairs over the broad marble staircase where an old wooden statue of a saint stood in the corner, with chipped and peeling paint. Upstairs, we entered through a double swinging glass door into her parents living quarters. "My mother, born a von Paschwitz, brought all this century-old furniture when they married and decorated my father's empty castle with them," Ella explained.

"Mother loves all these antiques. But Father calls it, 'dust-collecting junk'. He is a farmer now and doesn't care about all this nobility stuff she inherited."

We followed Ella through a long, dark hallway with a long side table, a large old painting hanging above it. "It's so dark in here, I can't see what's in the painting," Polli remarked, but Ella didn't answer and rushed us on. At the end of the hallway, we reached Tante Ruth's bright kitchen. It had a big window and a huge glass cabinet with lots of fine, gold-rimmed china and wine glasses, but only a little electric stove and no cooking utensils

"My mother doesn't like to cook, and our dinners with her friends from the nobility side of her family are prepared downstairs by Grandma," Ella explained with a touch of guilt in her face. "They all come here for a plentiful meal while other people are starving," Turning to the right she motioned us to go on.

"Now you'll see our great red parlor with a secret stairwell. You have to guess where it is. Father keeps his bootlegging secrets and other treasures in this hiding place. Our red salon has a little harem in its alcove, with everything imported from Turkey, where Father worked before the war. I love to hide in there on the soft pillows behind the wood-carved screen.

It's a good way to avoid doing chores. You know, if they don't see me, they can't give me work to do. Come on you'll see."

The burgundy-red brocade walls and draperies didn't impress Polli and me as much as the puzzle of the hidden stairwell. We started looking for it, tapping every foot along the wall. We searched behind every painting and examined the huge crystal framed-mirror above a heavy, old desk. Underneath, we saw sawdust from woodworms. Disappointed, we gave up our search, doubting if there was a hidden stairwell at all.

"I knew you wouldn't find it. Even the police couldn't find it when they raided the house last month. I guess they suspected Dad of doing something illegal. You can't see the door if you don't know about it, because it blends right in with the wallpaper." Ella opened a little door to a narrow spiral staircase leading down to the first floor. On each step, I saw containers standing next to one another and jars with clear liquid in them stood farther down. "Father makes his own brandy and hides it in here. You can't go in because it is so crammed full of stuff," Ella said while closing the door and stroking the loose wallpaper over it again.

We followed Ella through a wide French door, leading into Tante Ruth's charming, yellow-wallpapered living room. There were comfortable couches and upholstered armchairs in a light flower design. Along the walls stood bookshelves, a music chest with a radio and an old 'Telefunken' record player with a huge silvery funnel. I liked this light and friendly room right away.

"You two can sleep here on the big lounge chair in the alcove, or on the two couches in the red parlor," Ella remarked, making decisions as if she were the lady of the house. What a brat and a show-off, I thought.

"It would be so much more fun sleeping with you in your room. Where is it? We could have a pillow fight," Polli suggested.

"Oh no, I don't think so," Ella quipped. "My room is right next to mother's bedroom. Mother always sleeps long till nine o'clock and doesn't like to be disturbed. But I'll show you her bedroom right now while she is gone," Ella said, acting like the lady of the house again.

I don't remember much of Tante Ruth's bedroom except her king-size bed with a large painting of herself in the nude above it.

"Why would she have herself painted like that?" Polli asked looking at the painting.

"Oh, it was a famous painter who did it. You know, in art it's alright when you are naked," Ella lectured us, lifting her left shoulder and her nose.

"But where does Onkel Karl sleep?" Polli inquired.

"Oh, they don't sleep together anymore. Dad says he has to get up so early in the morning to go out to the fields. Now, since he has no more farm hands helping him, Olga, the Russian woman, helps him out in the barn during the day and in the house at night." Ella, the wise one, gave us a long look to check if we understood the hidden meaning.

"Dad's room is off-limits downstairs and so is Grandma's. Both are next to her kitchen. These rooms are a mess and we are not allowed to go there. Grandma collects and keeps everything. Her room is stuffed to the ceiling in the alcove. She can't throw anything away."

Turning towards us, Ella announced, "So this is the end of my guided tour. The third floor of the castle is now occupied by refugees, and we can't go there. But I can show you the stables with the horses and the cows. The barn is right next to the stable and we can go upstairs and jump in the hay. Come on, get going, what are you waiting for? I told you already, I don't have to ask for permission. I can do as I please."

Outdoors, the sun reflected on the water of the moat surrounding the castle. Dozens of white geese and even more ducks were peacefully lying in the grass. Suddenly Ella shouted, "Let's chase the geese and ducks back into the muddy water. Come on you two, don't be shy." Ella ran ahead, breaking a branch of one of the willow trees and ran towards the animals, screaming among the shrieking birds. We twins stood at the gravel road and watched our cousin in dismay.

In the stable, Ella fed hay to the two farm horses and fresh grass from a wheelbarrow to the cows, while Polli and I watched admiringly.

"Mother won a trophy last May in the steeplechase with her horse. She is at the equestrian show today," Ella explained, bragging.

Later, while we were in the loft of the barn having fun jumping in the hay, we heard a hard rumbling coming up the wooden stairs. Holding her hands in front of her mouth Ella said,

"Oh my God, it's our goat. He is very aggressive. His horns can hurt you badly. What shall we do now?" Not being used to farm animals, Polli and I looked scared at Ella. "Come on hurry, I'll show you an escape. It is dangerous and difficult but it will lead us to safety." She took us by the hand and showed us the escape route. I drew the shortest straw and had to crawl first. Slowly, inch by inch, we three girls crept on our bellies across a bearing beam underneath the loft floor boards. Frightened of the goat, the height and the cement floor below us, I dared not look down until I reached the other side of the beam and landed in Onkel Karl's arms.

"So, that's what you are up to. Nothing but mischief again, Ella! I'm sure it was your idea to let the goat out and scare the twins."

Onkel Karl sent Ella to her room and gave us each a big hug. He was blond, blue eyed and tall, with a muscular body and tanned skin. Onkel Karl was nice to us and laughed out loud when we told him about our adventures of the day. Polli and I liked Onkel Karl right away, especially after he took us on a hayride out to his fields and meadows.

In the evening, Tante Ruth came home, looking beautiful in her riding outfit. She was tall with black shiny hair turned up in a stylish twist and a china-doll white skin. We twins admired her. "Oh you are even more beautiful than in the painting in your bedroom," Polli acknowledged in surprise. Laughing, she said, "Ella showed you my bedroom? She was not allowed to do so. You two are so cute, and I don't mind being admired." Tante Ruth led us to her living room, serving us tea and heavenly-tasting cookies. "I hope you two girls will be a good influence on my Ella during these two weeks of you stay here with us," she said, while helping us make our bed in the alcove of her living room. Polli and I couldn't fall asleep for a long time, thinking of all the exciting things we experienced on our first day in Dolling.

Every day of our vacation brought new experiences for us girls. We drove with Onkel Karl on his tractor to the fields and rode on one of his farm horses. At sunset, we three girls chased the free-roaming geese and ducks into their wire enclosures. At first, Polli and I were afraid of these huge white geese with a hump above their beaks, but later we followed Ella jumping into the dirty water, splashing wildly and yelling loudly. Afterwards we fell exhausted onto the grass, not caring if there were green droppings from the animals.

One day, I had to feed the pig. As soon as I opened the latch of its wooden stall, that big monster jolted so hard against it that the whole enclosure shook. Scared, I dropped the pail with the potato peels and ran outside as fast as I could. To my further distress, Ella stood there watching and laughing.

The summer nights in Dolling were hot and humid. Polli and I couldn't fall asleep and brought our sleeping bags into the red parlor where we placed them right in front of two open windows. The windows swung back and forth in the light breeze, and the moonlight crept slowly across the carpet. Polli and I loved to sit next to one another, watching the silvery moon, the swaying willows and their shadows in the water of the moat. A thousand frogs sang a loud, croaking serenade and a dog barked in the village, joining the frog concert.

We wanted to prolong our last night in Dolling and enjoy these beautiful hours as long as we could stay awake. We twins felt sad to leave this beautiful place where we had so many new and delightful experiences.

27

Traveling to Northern Germany

Polli and I had our confirmation in the old Lutheran Church and considered ourselves almost grown up at age fourteen. A confirmation was an important event, and all the relatives came to celebrate. We had to learn the catechism and know what we were supposed to believe. Fifty boys and girls, dressed in formal black, walked in a long line up to the altar for the consecration.

Our confirmation presents were two new, burgundy-red bicycles and a trip with our mother to the North Sea. We twins never had anything brand new for as long as we could remember. We knew our mother worked long, hard hours at the quarry to save the money for such expensive presents.

Proud to own these beautiful bikes, Polli and I tried them out on a sandy country road the next day. Few people used this road, so we could learn how to ride a bike mostly unwatched. The first few timid minutes practicing were tough, but we kept trying until we felt confident enough to ride to the next village.

Riding our bikes in the cool spring air was so exhilarating, we both felt great. Excitedly, we worked the pedals faster and faster, racing one another. Happy about our accomplishment, we had no eyes for the pretty countryside, the wildflowers in the meadows or the new wheat seedlings sprouting in the nearby fields.

Turning around to see if Polli was still following me, I overlooked a big hole in the ground and fell foreword over the handlebar. Shock and fear paralyzed me in the first moments, so I didn't feel the pain on my knees and worried only about my bike. Is it broken? What will Mami say? Will I be punished for being so careless? What about the long bicycle trip

Mami planned to the North Sea and Hamburg? With my front wheel severely bent, we slowly walked back home, pushing our bikes along.

A week later my bike was repaired, and Mami, Polli and I lifted our bikes and climbed into the back of a canvas-covered truck that was carrying a load of marble slabs to Koblenz in the Rhineland. At work Mother had arranged for us to hitchhike with the truck. The long, hard ride lasted from morning till evening, with the three of us sitting on a thin layer of straw on top of the stones, our bicycles and backpacks next to us. Excited about our first trip to far away places, Polli and I didn't mind our sore bottoms. Looking out the open back of the truck, we enjoyed watching the busy highway traffic, especially the many old, gas-powered trucks with wood burning caldrons attached to the cab.

"Mami, why do they have stoves on the back of their trucks?" Polli expressed her amazement.

"Gasoline is still hard to get in our slowly recovering economy, so many trucks burn wood chips to power their trucks." Mother replied. A minute later, she pointed to a little, funny looking Messerschmitt car.

"Oh Mami, these cars are so low and have only three wheels, one in front and two in the back. I never saw anything like that," I expressed my observation to compete with Polli. "They look like toy cars with their round glass covers above the drivers. I have seen those on airplanes in grandfather's old pictures from World War I. Look Mami, there is only room for two people riding behind one another."

However, what we enjoyed most on this ride was Mami. She was so relaxed, unlike at home where she was often stressed from her work at the quarry. Now, Mami had time for us twins, hugging us to stay warm in the hold of the truck and telling us stories to shorten the long ride. She told us about the places we were going to see and the people we were going to meet.

We finally arrived in Koblenz ten hours later, hurting all over and walking stiff-legged like zombies. We all felt uneasy about spending the night with friends of friends we didn't know. Our mother had made these arrangements beforehand. Luckily, they were very nice people who invited us to sleep on mattresses in their living room. We were so happy staying in a private home because we were unable to pay for a hotel room in the bombed city. Although our hosts had little, they shared freely their food and local wine. Koblenz is located at the confluence of the river Mosel and the Rhine. We loved the beautiful location of the city and its old fortress 'Ehrenbachhoehe' high above.

After a good night's sleep, we all felt encouraged to continue our trip on a different truck. Our mother was invited to ride with the driver in the cab, and we girls sat down on several blankets in the empty cargo hold. I remember how the hours dragged on and on, with many short stops for us to jump out and stretch our legs. Back on the empty truck again, we girls sat huddled together in old blankets, shivering and cold. Now, Polli and I didn't feel so grown up anymore. We worried someone would climb into the back of the truck at one of the many stops. We wouldn't have known what to do in such an event. We imagined danger at every stop and felt so relieved when finally our truck arrived in the city of Bremen.

There, to our big surprise, Mother looked at us girls and admitted to us, "Let's hope we find the home of Onkel Hanni's friends among the ruins. I hope they still live at their old address. I didn't get an answer to my letter."

Luckily we received a warm welcome after finally finding the address. Like Onkel Hanni, they were also refugees from former East Prussia and lived cramped together in a small attic apartment. We didn't mind sleeping on the floor of their tiny kitchen. Next day, we had only a few hours of sightseeing in the old city of Bremen which was only partly destroyed in the war. We admired the beautiful gothic city hall with the tall statue of the legendary Roland in the plaza. We looked for the animal monument of the '*Bremer Stadtmusikanten*', my favorite Grimm fairy tale, but couldn't find it in the unfamiliar city.

"Now comes the fun part of our trip," Mother exclaimed happily the next morning. "We will ride our bicycles all the way to the city of Cuxhaven at the North Sea. You two will love it, the terrain is flat and we don't have to labor up steep mountains like back home in Bavaria."

Encouraged, we started our biking trip. Most of the time, I rode my bike behind Mother and Polli, hoping they would see the potholes in the road. My fall from the bike at home had taught me a lesson, and I was still unsure of my bike riding ability.

We rode through beautiful countryside, with meadows and grazing black and white '*Holstein*' cows. We passed many red brick and timber-framed farmhouses with straw roofs and lots of flowers in every front yard. Red, wild poppies enlivened the yellow of the ripening wheat fields.

"Look, Mami, there is a big wagon wheel on the roof of that house," I called out pointing up.

Polli joined in with another discovery, "Mami look, there is a stork in a big straw nest on top of another wheel. We never saw anything like that at home."

Mother didn't answer but shouted, "Watch out! There is a ditch in the road. Be careful or you'll fall again. Look around and you will see things are different here, and most people living in this province of Holstein are blond and blue-eyed."

"Yeah, and they speak a strange dialect, I can't understand at all. Sounds, almost like a bunch of ducks quaking." Polli remarked, laughing.

"Oh, Polli, what a funny girl you are," Mother said, laughing too. "The dialect here in the far north of Germany is called '*Plattdeutsch*'. It's an old dialect, and it has more Dutch and English than German words.

In the city of Cuxhaven, we had our first glimpse of the North Sea, with the surf pounding against the breakwater. Excited, we rode closer to get a better look. Riding on a narrow, tall dike, I felt so insecure with water so close on each side of the dam. The green, fishy-smelling North Sea wasn't what I had expected from pictures of an azure sky and deep-blue water. "Do people like to swim in this?" I asked Mother.

When we entered the city of Cuxhaven, we saw lots of rundown dirty warehouses and a harbor filled with smelly fishing boats. There was a heavy fog, partly disguising the disappointing sight. I was not impressed and wondered why Mother wanted to come to a smelly place like this.

After leaving Cuxhaven, we spent the night in a lone farmhouse in the country. The old house had a straw roof, and a stable was attached in the back. I didn't like the smell of sour milk penetrating every room from the big milk pails near the cow's stable and couldn't fall asleep for a long time.

Next day, we headed south along the shore of the impressive River Elbe. We enjoyed bicycling on a country road next to this sparkling, wide waterway with lots of smoke-puffing ships.

"This river is the main waterway from Germany's biggest port in Hamburg to the North Sea," Mother explained.

"We know all that" I answered. "We learned it in school, but I thought it would look different, prettier, more exciting.

Forty miles south of Cuxhaven, we took the ferry to cross the Elbe at Pinneberg and rode through miles and miles of fields filled with roses of all shades and colors.

"Look at all these beautiful roses! There are so many different kinds, and they grow in such long rows all the way to the horizon," Polli called out, and we stepped from our bikes to enjoy the gorgeous sight and pungent smell.

"Holstein is famous not only for its white and black cows and milk products but also for the rose plantations. Roses from these farms are shipped all over Germany and to some neighboring countries."

Late afternoon we arrived in Hamburg, the second-largest city in Germany. The city had been bombed heavily in the war and was only partly rebuilt in its center. In most areas of the city, the rubble and ruins had been cleared away, and a vast expanse of flat land with only streets and posts with street names were visible. We three tired bikers searched for a long time till we finally found the street where our friends supposedly lived. We looked around, but there were no houses left standing for a mile or so.

"But I just received a letter from them," Mother said, wondering. Standing there dumbfounded and not knowing what to do, a mailman on a bicycle told us, "People here live in their basements and cellars underground. The address you are looking for is just a hundred meters farther."

We knocked at Krueger's cellar door and were greeted warmly by an old woman with thin gray hair, yellow skin and deep shadows under her eyes. One could see she had experienced lots of hardship as a refugee from East Prussia.

"Come in, please! My daughter and son are working in the city. They will be home soon. I have been expecting you and will warm up a potato soup. I cooked a piece of smoked ham with it and lots of marjoram."

Looking around the big cellar room where the whole Krueger family lived and slept, we felt we couldn't impose and ask to spend the night with them. While the old woman went to a corner to tend to the soup, Polli whispered to Mother, "I saw a poster sign of the big sailing ship Pamir, anchored in Hamburg harbor for the summer. It serves as a youth hostel, and if we hurry we may still get a cabin. Wouldn't that be exciting, sleeping on a real sailing ship? I'm sure you can stay with us, Mami!"

Over soup, Mami told the nice old woman about our plan, and we noticed she was relieved to hear we did not plan to stay with her family over night.

The big port of Hamburg was full of luxury liners and freighters of all sorts. For us three Bavarians, it was especially exciting to see all the activity of a busy harbor with so many cranes, ships and tugboats. Speechless, we stood at the pier, admiring the Pamir. She was one of the few tall ships left from the old sailing regatta. The Pamir was remarkably clean and beautiful, boasting a polished mahogany wood deck. Her masts stretched so high, we could hardly see the tops. We felt like in a dream when we got a cabin with three cots for two nights. In Hamburg, we learned a lot about sailing and a sailor's life, especially when we walked along a street at night called '*Reeperbahn*'.

"*Reeperbahn* is a typical harbor street in *Sankt Pauli* (a district in the city) with sailor hang-outs, pubs, brothels and other amusements. You are fourteen now and you may as well learn and understand this side of a sailor's life," Mother explained to us girls. We passed garish advertisements in stalls, shops and brothels with half-dressed women in the windows on this brightly illuminated street.

Two people turned around when Polli loudly asked, "Mami, why is the *Reeperbahn* famous? I can't see any nice places here and there are so many people strolling along the sidewalks, one can hardly pass them. Do sailors like this dump of a street?"

The last night of our long trip, we stayed again on the Pamir. The sailing vessel was anchored in a quiet corner of the harbor. We enjoyed listening to the slapping of the waves against the hull and the sound of the wind in the rigging until we finally fell asleep around midnight.

We took an old, steam-powered train back home with the last Deutsch Marks Mother had saved for our tickets. We boarded the train half an hour early to make sure to get good seats and had time on the long ride back to relax and reflect on our experiences during our two-week journey. The train was crowded with all kinds of people; tired mothers with screaming children and handicapped men with guide dogs. In addition to all these people, there were crates, boxes and suitcases crammed into the compartments of the old-fashioned wagons. It was a long train ride back through most of West Germany until we arrived in Solnhofen, but is was a lot more comfortable than the truck rides on the way north.

We were glad to be home again and talked excitedly about our trip by truck, bicycle and train, our great adventure we will never forget.

28

Lyceum-High School Years

Going to an all-girl high school from 1950 to 1953 had its positive and negative sides. For Polli and me, it was the best way for a higher education. Our High school, or our lyceum as it was called at the time, was not located in our hometown Solnhofen. We had to take the train leaving Solnhofen at seven in the morning, to be in Treuchtlingen when school started at eight o'clock. Often leaving our house in the last minute, we ran to the station and took a shortcut through the old cemetery to catch the train. In the late afternoon, after school ended, we dawdled on our twenty-minute walk to the train station, making detours to avoid the tunnel, where more than 250 people had died in an air raid in World War II.

Our school was also heavily bombed in the same air raid and was being renovated during our first year in school. The three-storied building still had lots of broken windows, some of them covered with cardboard. During the first winter, we students sat in the classrooms dressed in coats to stay warm.

Although I had studied hard for the important entrance examination, I had failed the test in mathematics. Bad school experiences with a tyrannical teacher in elementary school made me nervous during these tests. Polli, on the other hand did well in the entrance exam. Being Polli's identical twin, the teachers decided to let me enter the privileged school anyway. I was lucky not to be separated from my sister and hoped to prove to the teachers that I could do as well as the other students.

From our first day in school, the faculty treated us as a twin team rather than as two individual persons. We didn't mind in the beginning; after all, we were used to it. However, as time passed, we wanted to be seen and counted as Hertha and Paula. We grew to dislike being stereotyped as an inseparable unit.

I liked being allowed to sit next to Polli in each classroom. The teachers usually didn't mind, because we both did well in most subjects. However, in math class Polli often whispered to me to make sure I had the right answers to the problems. Frau Kremer, our shortsighted principal, didn't like our whispering. Squinting with her eyes, she pushed her glasses up to her forehead and waddled close to us twins, trying to tell us apart.

"Which one of you is Hertha, and which one is Paula", she demanded to know, standing next to us. On most occasions in the past she had guessed and missed, to the laughter of the whole class. Walking back to the front of the class room she muttered to herself, "No matter which one I pick "both of you always give me the same answer." Frau Kremer stopped her investigation after the first few tries.

Teenaged Twins

Fraeulein Assessor (initial rank of teacher) was our English language teacher. She had been severely injured in an air attack and her face was distorted with big scars and deep-red blotches. We didn't learn much in her class because most students constantly interrupted her lessons, teasing her, calling her ugly or making noises so nobody could hear her voice. The disfigured woman felt insecure and couldn't control our class. When things got too bad, she started crying and left the room. Then the noise got even louder till the principal arrived. Polli and I felt bad every time this happened, in particular because we didn't stand up against the instigators and troublemakers.

Our favorite teacher was Frau *Studienrat* (advanced rank of teacher) Lebherz, an always properly dressed lady in her forties with very white skin, hazel brown eyes and black hair. Polli and I admired her demeanor, her style and her quiet way of talking. No one in her grammar and literature class would dare to interrupt. She inspired me to be interested in literature and read classical books ever since.

Herr Schwab was our music teacher and the only male on the faculty. Several girls in our class thought he was a most interesting and good-looking man. Polli and I didn't agree, but we liked his teaching. His enthusiasm for music was contagious. We all loved to sing in his school choir, and after we won the state championship we liked it even more. For his most interested students, Herr Schwab bought tickets for the opera in Nuremberg and introduced us to operatic and classical music.

I still remember how excited I was at the concert of Elli Ney, one of Germany's well-known pianists at the time. The tall, white-haired lady, dressed in black, played Beethoven's "*Waldstein Sonata*" so marvelously, we twins kept talking about it for days. Our first opera was "Madame Butterfly" by Puccini. Herr Schwab introduced us students beforehand to the plot and the music structure. It was an unforgettable performance, and we twins enjoy opera since then.

Soon, Polli and I became good friends with the classmates who rode the same train to school and back to their home towns in late afternoon. These girls accepted and treated us as individuals, a fact particularly appreciated by Polli. Three of our classmates lived in Pappenheim, the town one train stop before ours. These girls were great fun to be with. They came from well-to-do families and still had fathers at home. Since we didn't, we envied them for having a father who took care of them. We often liked to spend time with them in Pappenheim, hiking up to the ruins of the old castle or collecting wild mushrooms in the forest.

One evening I told Mother, "Mami, on the train there was an old man obviously listening in on our conversation. We five schoolgirls didn't like it and told him so, but he just kept listening and smiling. What a nasty old guy. Mami, what should we do in such a case?"

Wondering, our mother asked, "How old, do you think, was this 'old man'?"

"Oh I don't know, maybe forty." When I looked at my mother her whole body jiggled, and her mouth showed an amused smile, she tried to conceal. "What's so funny?" I asked.

"Oh my dear, at forty a man isn't old," Mother said laughingly.'

"But you know what? Regardless of how old the man was, he couldn't help hearing what you five girls were talking about sitting in the same compartment. I wouldn't make anything of him listening in".

One day Ella Grimm, one of our new friends from school, invited us to a sleepover. She was a skinny blonde with watery eyes. She and her family were refugees from Prussia and lived in an apartment in the new castle of Pappenheim. Polli and I thought it must be exciting to live in a castle of a former count, especially one with a famous ancestor from the seventeenth century! This count and his soldiers in the *Thirty-Year War* were known to be particularly courageous and reliable, so his superior general coined the proverb, "Ich kenne meine Pappenheimer" (I know my Pappenheim people/soldiers).

After sunset, we played ghosts in our nightgowns, with our bed sheets over our heads, running along the halls of the castle and down its wide tread-bare staircase to the old park. The silvery moon looked like a lantern, hanging on the crooked old willow tree, and its light sparkled in the water of the Altmuehl river. Halloween was not known in Germany at the time, but Polli and I felt so spooky when Ella opened the rusty, creaking door to the centuries-old tomb of the Pappenheim Counts. She whispered to us, "Don't wake the dead in the tomb. The famous count, however, isn't buried here. His grave is in the church next door, with a heavy stone plate on top of it, so his ghost can't escape." Scared, in this creepy tomb, Polli and I ran outside screaming, looking not like ghosts but like two very frightened girls. Some neighbors, who came out to see what the noise was all about, laughed and tried to scare us even more with their remarks. "Look out you girls, the ghost of the old count is following you!"

During these years, textbooks from the Nazi era were not to be used in school and new books were not yet available for students. Only teachers had a few of these new textbooks that they read to the students aloud while the students were taking notes. We all learned shorthand to follow the teachers' reading. Later at home, we transferred the shorthand notes in handwriting to our journals. This was very time-consuming; but we learned many of the subjects already by writing them twice.

The three years of schooling in the Lyceum in Treuchtlingen were not only enjoyable and stimulating for Polli and me, but they profoundly affected our lives in the future. We only appreciated in later years that the excellence and compassion of several of our teachers had shaped our young minds and laid the foundation for our developing interests.

29

Our Hometown Solnhofen

During our childhood, Solnhofen was a small town of about 2000 inhabitants. It is located in the picturesque Altmuehl river valley, surrounded by the mountains of the Fraenkische Jura. The site of a church and cloister, founded in the 7th and 8th centuries by monks, the town grew to its present size, predominantly due to the lime stone industry, during the last two hundred years.

The river separates the town into the old part on the shadowy west side and the newer part on the sunny east side. There is a Lutheran and a Catholic church, a town hall, an elementary school, a couple of hotels and a bank. Our grandmother's house is located in "old town", near the town hall. My grandfather, one of the quarry owners and mayors of Solnhofen, bought the house in the early 20th century. It is built in the "Gruenderstil", a somewhat ornamental architecture, popular at that time.

Solnhofen Looking East across the Altmuehl River

When I grew up, my grandfather had died and our family lived with Grandmother and her sister Tante Marie in this stately house. From our windows, we looked across the river to the east side of town, with slowly rising slopes up to a flat plateau. Most houses reached from the valley up the sunny slopes of the plateau. In contrast, on the shady westside, the mountains rose high and were covered with beech and pine trees. High above on some mountain ridges, one could see the light-gray *"Schutthalden"* (slate dumping mounts) from the quarries.

"Solnhofer Platten", often called Jura marble, were very popular as a floor and wall covering and also essential for lithographic printing. Most of the men in Solnhofen worked in the quarries up on the mountains while the women did all the work in and around their homes.

The houses of the stone-workers' families were small, with little windows, and the roofs were covered with slate-tiles from the limestone quarries. Working in the open quarries was hard for the men, being exposed to the hot sun in the summer and the cold and snow in the winter. On their way home on Fridays, the men usually dropped in at the pubs to quench their thirsts. Solnhofen had seven taverns where the stoneworkers used to spend much or all of their weekly wages before coming home, drunk, to their angry wives. We kids loved to watch the spectacle every Friday evening, when some women dragged their drunken and complaining husbands out of the taverns.

During the war years and afterwards, our mother didn't have much time for us twin girls. Our school hours were from eight in the morning till noon on weekdays and Saturdays. After our homework and daily duties had been done, we twins had lots of time on our own to play and roam around in the little town or up on the mountains in its limestone quarries and in the woods.

One daily job was to carry our neighbor's Mr. Huettinger freshly cooked lunch up the mountain to his stone manufacturing plant above the quarry. While there, we observed how the workers cut, split and polished the plates of limestone called "Jura Marble". The scrap and broken pieces were hauled away to big heaps. Years later, the rejected pieces were ground and used for making cement.

We children loved to search around these dumps for little fossils of fishes, crabs, snails, or some nice pieces of limestone with flower-like designs in brown and gray shades. We had quite a collection of these slates in our hiding place in the woods above our house. When we asked questions about these fossils of strange looking fishes with long beaks and many little teeth, Mother said, "They are petrified fishes about one-hundred-fifty million years old," Although we couldn't imagine how much so many million years would be, we knew these fossils were very, very old.

"But why are there petrified fishes in our mountains?" Polli and I wondered, asking Mother.

"That's because an ocean covered the land around here millions of years ago. Actually, it was only a large, shallow lagoon at the edge of an ancient ocean," Mother explained while going to get a book. That was her way to get us to learn from books when we were interested in a certain subject. She handed us a book with many pictures, graphs and easy explanations. This book and a museum visit were the beginning of our interest to find out more about fossils.

In the fossil museum of Eichstaett, we girls saw fossilized four-to five-foot long fishes, equally big snails and huge dragonflies. We learned about many species becoming extinct, and others still living today, although in a much smaller versions. The biggest excitement for us thirteen-year-olds was a rare and very valuable fossil in a glass cage all by itself. It showed a bird with long feathers on its tail and wings. "They call him *Archaeopterix*. It was the first species of birds ever to be on earth, and it had developed from a small dinosaur, about the size of a turkey" the guide explained to us girls.

When we were children we knew little about the local history of Solnhofen. We played hide and seek among the ruins of the Sola Basilica next to the old cloister. Nobody hindered us girls from playing there, where the weeds grew between the floor tiles and from the cracks in the walls. The ruins of the former basilica had no roof anymore, yet the north aisle with several stone columns was still standing. We knew the little house-like block with no windows or doors was called the tomb of Saint Sola, the Irish monk who founded Solnhofen. We also knew the ruins were from an old church built in the early Middle-Ages. We enjoyed hiding behind the colonnade of columns with the beautiful stone carvings on top.

Today, these ruins are an important archeological site, covered with a wide roof and surrounded by a fence. Ten years ago, on one of my occasional visits to Solnhofen, I learned that in 1976 archeologists found the remains of three older churches below the basilica. The basilica was built in 820 AD, but the remnants of the oldest church go back to 650 AD. I didn't know Christianity had already existed in Germany as early as the 7th Century. Like most Germans, I thought the country was Christianized during the reign of Charlemagne about 800 AD.

During the first three centuries A.D., Germanic tribes migrated into the area around the upper Danube River, which was occupied by Romans and Celtic tribes. At that time, Christianity coexisted with the old pagan beliefs. After many battles, the Franks, a Germanic tribe from the north, took over this area and fully Christianized the country under the reign of Charlemagne.

Sola founded Sola-Hofen (Sola's Place) in 750 AD on a land grant from Charlemagne, who had come up the river Altmühl by boat from the Danube. Charlemagne was surveying the land for a canal he wanted to build to connect the Danube with the Rhine and thereby the Atlantic Ocean with the Black Sea. Charlemagne ruled over a vast area of now central Europe. He knew that transport of goods on waterways would increase trade tremendously in the still wild Germanic land. Near the remains of the *"Fossa Carolina,"* Charlemagne's never finished canal, archeologists found even older ruins from a Roman villa with beautifully preserved mosaic floors, a steam bath and many artifacts.

We twins were excited to learn about the colorful history of Solnhofen and the area around it in high school. As children we knew Celts used to live in the area, because we were familiar with the Celtic names of some places, such as *"Drudenbuck"*, a hill where the religious leaders of the Celts (Druids) convened. One of our favorite Celtic places to play was on top of the *"Teufelskanzel"* (Devils-Altar, so named by the Christians later). We climbed this huge cubic monolith, crowning a cone-shaped, almost treeless mountain. Polli and I loved to pick flowers there. We placed them into a water puddle that formed in a hollow on top of the rock after it had rained. We pretended we were pagan Celts, offering flowers and looking out for enemies from our high observation post. Many years later, we learned archeologists had found in a dig nearby an ancient Celtic brooch, two glass rings and a bronze bracelet among many broken spears.

In a prominent place in the middle of "old-town" Solnhofen stands a monument with a life-size statue of Alois Senefelder. We children knew that he was the inventor of lithography, a new printing method yielding outstanding print quality. We also knew he developed this new printing method in Solnhofen over two hundred years ago. From that time on, Solnhofen's thick, heavy lithography stones have been used all over the world. Polli and I liked looking at the life-size statue of Senefelder, wondering, how he got the idea to search here in our town for the right stone he needed for his new printing method. Years later, I found out that high-quality lithography requires the use of very fine-grained limestone, found especially in the area where Solnhofen is located.

The outside appearance of Solnhofen has not changed much since my childhood. There are some new modern one-family houses up in the hills on the east side, but the rest of the town remains pretty much the same. However, Solnhofen has become a quiet place, especially in the evenings when people sit in front of their television screens. Also, in the fifty-five years since I left the town, the population has changed to a mix of Germans and immigrants from Turkey, Romania and other countries.

The stone business has not been doing well for many years. People shop and work in other towns where the jobs are, but they still live in Solnhofen. Many shops have closed down, and there is only one tavern left. Even that is almost empty, except for some tourists that have come to enjoy the newly established *"Naturpark Altmühltal."*

Yet, whenever I visit Solnhofen, long forgotten memories of my childhood come back. In search of my past, I walk to the places of my childhood to see if they are still the same. I am happy when they are and disappointed but understanding when they are not, knowing very well that nothing stays the same in life.

Winter in Our Hometown Solnhofen Looking West

30

Our Best Friend

Mrs. Adele Will was a lady only a few years younger than our grandmother. Polli and I were at ease with her, we could talk to her, we loved listening to her, and she always had time for us. She was different from most people in our town, and so were we.

Our friendship started way back during the last year of the war, when we were children, about nine years old. One day, Mrs. Will came to our house to borrow some books from Mother's library. She loved children and found us shy, cute twin girls especially likable.

During that first visit, she invited Polli and me to a children's party at the apartment the Wills had rented. We girls were surprised, that a lady, who didn't know us, would invite us to a party. Our mother knew the Will family had came to Solnhofen in 1943 from Berlin. Mother was glad for us girls and had no objection to let us go to the party. We twins were happy and wondered no longer about the lady's reasons.

When we entered her apartment, Polly and I blurted out, "Mrs. Will, we didn't know you live in the house of our mother's cousin!"

"Well, children, if I had known that myself, I would have told you about it", Mrs. Will answered. "What a real surprise!

She led us into her dining room furnished with Chippendale furniture. Three children our age had also been invited. In the middle of the room stood a beautifully set table with lots of cookies, a delicious cake topped with strawberries and lots of whipped cream. Staring at these delicatessens made our eyes grow wide and our mouths water. Delicious food like this was never served at our house. Nor could one buy such food in stores, and Mother had little to trade with the farmers. We were always hungry during those years, and a strawberry cake with whipped cream was like a dream come true.

Adele Will, we always called her Mrs. Will, the polite form to address a lady, was a five foot, somewhat heavy set woman in her fifties with a friendly face and ash-blond, curly hair, already partly graying. She wore thick glasses over her gray eyes and had an unusually high forehead. She was not a good-looking woman, but we liked her warmth, her optimism and her humor. We were invited many more times by Mrs. Will after her family moved next door to their newly built house. Polly and I grew very fond of her in the years to come. Her interest in music, books and the arts were instrumental in developing the same interests in us.

Although she had suffered through terrible nights of bombings in Berlin, she kept her positive attitude and her love for life and children. Mrs. Will moved with her two sons from Berlin to Solnhofen in 1943, at the time still a peaceful little town. Her husband remained with his business in Berlin during weekdays until a few months before the end of the war. Weekends he spent often with his family in Solnhofen. The Wills also had a daughter, about 10 years older than the sons. She studied music at the Vienna Conservatory.

Even after her husband joined his family in Solnhofen, we saw little of him when we visited Mrs. Will. He spent much of his time traveling and building new business relationships. In addition, he was busy getting acquainted with farmers to exchange, machines and tools from his business for food to feed his family.

We girls also rarely saw Mrs. Will's two sons, five and eight years older than us. They went to high school in Eichstaett, a city fifteen miles south of Solnhofen. The two boys were busy with their activities and their friends. Polli and I were happy to be with Mrs. Will and never missed not talking to her family. Being children, we enjoyed the extra time and attention Mrs. Will gave us; she always had some goodies for us and tried to do things with us we enjoyed.

The years passed and when we visited Mrs. Will, we always spent a lot of time at the piano, singing German folksongs and songs by Schubert, Schumann and other composers. Mrs. Will was a romantic, and so were Polli and I. We appreciated these musical afternoons at her house, because Mother no longer had time to sing with us at the piano, as she used to do before the war.

When Mrs. Will spoke about the "Good Old Times" in Ründeroth before World War I, her eyes lit up, and she looked so happy, remembering these times in her youth.

"You know, when I was your age, I joined the "Wandervogel" association. In this popular group, many boys and girls went hiking in the countryside, singing folksongs and having fun at picnics. All of us loved nature and the outdoors in our beautiful mountainous countryside, fifty miles east of Cologne."

On another occasion, Mrs. Will gave us a lively rendering of her first secret affection and later love for the brother of her best girl friend. "I spent a lot of time at my friend's, Millie Schluckebier, house and saw her older brother many times. He was a teacher at our elementary school. Sometimes, he sat down with us, and the three of us had animated discussions. He was such a charming and entertaining young man. I adored him and developed a crush for him. However, I don't believe, he ever knew about my feelings for him", she said with a chuckle in her voice.

Polli and I enjoyed the glimpse we got into the time just after the turn of the twentieth century. It seemed like such a different world, so peaceful and romantic! We were sad we had to grow up during and after devastating World War II.

Mrs. Will, as we kept addressing her, also gave us many books to read, mostly books her two sons had already read or out-grown. We liked to read the Karl May and James Fennimore Cooper books about the American Indians. Cooper's *"Lederstrumpf"* (Leather Stocking) tales of life during the 17th Century in Up-State New York we found especially exciting, never imagining that many years later I would live in the area where these adventures took place.

Three years after the war, the Will family moved from their rented apartment into a three-story house they had bought during the war and extensively rebuilt. Their family of five-their daughter had moved from Vienna to Solnhofen just before the end of the war-occupied the two lower floors, and they rented the third floor out to two other families. Mr. Will also maintained an office on the second floor of the spacious building. Before leaving Berlin early in 1945, Mr. Will had still managed to have the rest of their furniture transported to Solnhofen where it was kept in storage until it was used to furnish their own home.

When Polli and I visited Mrs. Will in their new home for the first time, we felt like we were stepping into a different world. A huge, forty by twenty foot room on the first floor was filled with heavy antique Renaissance and Chippendale furniture. Brocade draperies decorated the windows and original oil paintings hung on the walls.

Looking at our inquisitive faces, Mrs. Will explained, "Oh, you wonder about all the furniture? All our living room, dining room and music room furniture is in this one big room now. In Berlin, this furniture was spread out over three separate rooms. It looked very formal. My husband wanted to impress his business visitors. But here in Solnhofen, we thought it would be nicer to have one 'great room' where our family can be together. For working and sleeping, everybody has his or her own room."

Later, in the early fifties, we twins spent more time with Mrs. Will to help her get over the loss of her husband who had died suddenly in 1952. We went on long walks along the Altmühl river listening to her stories of times gone by or had the traditional coffee and cake in the afternoon. During the long twilight hours in the winter, we enjoyed classical music from her large record collection. Her friendly, optimistic way was contagious and we learned to like her even more as the years went by.

During our high school years, we had only time to visit Mrs. Will on weekends. Sometimes, her sons Fritz and Hanns came home on the same weekend. Being five and eight years older, they showed no interest in us sixteen-year-old girls, nor did we have any interest in them. Jokingly, they called us "their mother's little girls," and had fun teasing us, knowing we were shy and didn't know how to debate them. Angry over our inability, Polli and I tried to avoid them when they were around. However, with time, we started losing our shyness and learned to return their teasing remarks with proper answers. During those years, Fritz-the younger of the two-studied physics in Munich and Hanns studied business in Nuremberg. Often, when they came home Fritz brought his friends or girlfriends along from Munich.

"Oh, I like it when my boys bring their friends home so I can see whom they socialize with. Fritz always had girlfriends, even way back in Berlin, when he was in third grade. One time, my cleaning woman found a love letter in his clothes when she took them to the laundry. Eager little Fritz wanted to make sure he would get what he wanted and wrote, 'Dear Lola, choose me instead of Lemmerz, because he is a Catholic.' This was typical for blond and curly-haired, little Fritz." Adele laughed and, turning close to us girls, she whispered, "He loves girls and knows how to charm them."

When we were eighteen, we had attended business school and were looking for our first jobs. We were prepared to move to a larger city and felt excited when we both found two fascinating positions in Nuremberg in the same company, Photo Porst.

We still kept visiting Adele Will after we moved to Nuremberg. She was always glad to see us and usually had something special for us. She knew we liked Peach Melba, a dessert she could prepare particularly well.

Through all these years while we were growing up Polli and I always liked to be with Adele Will and enjoyed her friendship, never having the slightest idea, she would become my mother-in-law many years later.

31

Unreturned Love

At fifteen years of age, my twin sister and I were not interested in flirting and dating boys like so many of the girls in our high school. Most girls there were talking about their first crush on a boy, or how the guys would flirt with them. Polli and I didn't care about flirting and dating. We twins were happy to have each other and a loving mother and felt we didn't need another person in our close relationship. We loved to go to the movies and an occasional concert together or read, swim, ski, hike, and ride our bicycles together. Often, we liked to watch people and discussed our impressions and thoughts about them afterwards.

Polli and I never had fights, like most siblings do, and we were convinced this would also be the case with other identical twins. We read news articles about twins and medical studies about their similarities. We found ours was a perfect twin relationship. However, once in a while we disagreed, mostly when Polli tried to wear my dresses. "Mother made them look alike, but your dress makes you appear slimmer," she insisted.

"But Polli, you are perspiring under you arms, and I don't like to wear your smelly dresses."

We liked our harmonious twin life and planned never to separate, fall in love, nor get married. Most books we read were German literature classics, tragedies like Goethe's "*Faust.*" In those books, love always had tragic endings, mostly for the women or girls in it, who were either raped, or left alone by their lovers. We teenagers decided we didn't want to deal with love and the heartache that often seemed to follow. The few boys we had met we found silly. They made bets among each other which one of their group would be able to tell us apart, or get a date with one of us. They never were lucky, and we never cared about one, or any of them. Men were a mystery to us, because growing up during World War II without a father or grandfather, in a house with only women and children, Polli and I had no idea how men felt, nor acted in real life. Our experience with men came only from reading books.

One day, my five years younger sister Brigitte's teacher came to the house to talk to Mother about a special talent he had observed in her daughter. When he entered our living room, I was playing the piano and Polli was doing homework. To be polite and not to overhear their discussion, we withdrew to the unheated kitchen next door. After he left, Mother surprised us saying, "I made an appointment for us all to go on a nature hike with Mr. Keil next Saturday."

"But Mami we don't know this man and are not interested!" Polli and I shouted angrily together. "We have other plans for that day."

"Sorry, I made a commitment and I can't change it now. Besides, Mr. Keil can teach you something; he knows a lot about nature. He is really an interesting and nice man."

Polli and I were upset, Mother didn't ask us beforehand. We tried all kinds of excuses to avoid this hike but realized Mother wouldn't change the appointment. Angrily, Polli complained again, "Mother, why do you make arrangements for us? Why should we go on a nature hike with a man we have absolutely no interest in?"

The following Saturday morning, the teacher stood in front of our house. Mother opened the door and said, "I'm sorry, Mr. Keil. I have some unexpected work to do, but you and the girls can go on the hike."

"What a dirty trick," Polli shouted at Mother when she returned to us in the kitchen and told us that she was not coming along and wanted us to go alone with Mr. Keil who was still standing at the front door. From Mother we transferred our anger to Mr. Keil who had suggested the nature walk in the first place. "All right, if he is our little sister's teacher, why doesn't he go on a nature walk with his class of little children? I don't like to go on a hike with a man I don't know", Polli argued. But Mother would not listen and gave us no choice.

Later on the nature walk, Polli and I didn't speak for a long time, dragging our feet while walking next to the teacher. With side-glances, we kept inspecting the tall and slender man with blond, short-cut hair.

Fritz Keil was about ten years older than we. As a teacher he knew how to overcome a situation with two mute teenagers. Not being bothered by our silent resistance, he showed us rare flowers and birds we would not otherwise have seen. He saw things in nature most people overlooked. In the old limestone quarry, unused for several decades, he found fossils of little fishes millions of years old. Gradually impressed by his knowledge we didn't mind his long lecture about the Jurassic Age and the many animals living at the time in our area. After awhile he encouraged us to talk about our hobbies and interests. We entered into a long conversation and, to our surprise, found this three-hour nature walk wasn't so bad after all.

The following weekend, Mr. Keil was at the door again asking if we twins would go on another hike. He suggested a beautiful romantic trail along the Altmuehl River with many more interesting things to show us. We declined the offer, for we had a school outing that day.

However, this did not discourage Mr. Keil. He kept coming back to our house. One time, he needed to talk to Mother about Brigitte again. Another time, he came to borrow a special book he had seen in our bookcase. Every time, the man came, he had some suggestions about what he liked to show Polli and me. We went with him on another interesting hike. This time, the teacher showed us places farther away and told us a lot about their history we didn't know.

Another time, he suggested an art show he thought we would like. One weekend, he offered to try out a new vegetarian restaurant with us. We accepted and learned about the many special meals vegetarians prefer to eat. Naïve as we were at the time, we didn't suspect anything and Mother was glad the teacher liked to spend time with us for she was so overworked. She was glad when friends of hers, or our neighbors, invited us teenagers to come along with them for short sightseeing trips.

Polli and I grew more and more tired of going out with our sister's teacher. We made excuses until we ran out of them. I became suspicious of his motives, especially when he started to look so strangely at me, when he was together with Polli and me. I told Mother about my suspicions and asked to help us twins to get rid of him, but she declined, thinking the teacher was just trying to be nice. "Oh, you are imagining things, reading so many books." Frustrated with Mother's shrugging off my worries, Polli and I planned things to do with our school friends every Saturday and refused to see Mr. Keil. When he still kept coming to our house and offering to do things with us twins, we became angry at him and at Mother for not helping.

Some weeks later Mr. Keil came to the house during my cooking lesson at Grandma's kitchen upstairs. Polli and I took turns every Sunday, learning to cook. That day I learned how to cook a typical Sunday meal with a pork roast, potato dumplings, red cabbage and a green salad with chives. When I saw who was at the door, I didn't go downstairs to answer it. "Grandmother, I don't like that man. Will you talk with him?" Grandmother returned, saying, "I invited Mr. Keil to be our guest for lunch. The poor bachelor will love a good meal." What could I do? It was too late to run away or tell Grandmother that he was actually a vegetarian. The man, whom by now I disliked very much, had dinner with us in our house, against my wishes.

Mr. Keil acted like the perfect gentleman, giving compliments to my cooking and Grandma's beautiful Rosenthal china. When he remarked at the door how pretty I looked in an apron, I turned red in the face and felt so uncomfortable, wishing myself far away.

Some weeks later, I saw the teacher at a funeral. He came over and spoke to me in front of my school friends, embarrassing me no end. Another time, he suddenly appeared in front of me on my way up Black Mountain. How did he know I was there alone? I wondered. He always seemed to know were I was, or where I was planning to go. Was my little sister telling him? His constant stares and the way he talked and acted so strangely made me feel uneasy. I became afraid of him. By now, it was clear this man had a crush on me. But why me, I wondered. Why not my sister Polli? Why didn't he select a girl his age rather than a fifteen-year old? I was a shy girl and didn't know what to say to him to get out of this unpleasant situation politely. I couldn't tell him face to face that I was afraid of him. I felt awful about my inability to tell him off. Mother and Grandmother thought I was imagining things when I told them my suspicion, and they didn't help.

Only Polli knew how upset and afraid I was of Keil, so we designed a plan to get rid of him. Polli had less scruples to confront him, and together we felt more powerful to tell him, we didn't like nature walks anymore or any other meetings with him. However, our effort didn't work, and he kept appearing when I least expected it. For many weeks the man kept stalking me. Frustrated, I begged Mother, "Mami, please help me. Ask him to stop following me. He will listen to you, I'm sure of it." I felt easier, when we finally convinced Mother about Keil's real intentions. Finally she wrote him the requested letter, telling him, I was far too young for any love relationship and to leave me alone. Polli and I felt so relieved when he stopped bothering us and thought we had our twin life and peace of mind again.

However, four years later, Keil came back into our lives. Polli and I had graduated from high school and business-college. We now lived and worked in Nuremberg. We felt so happy to have our own little apartment, after two years with our old, well-meaning aunt Paula. She mothered us girls more than our mother ever did. We now felt grown up and independent and disliked her constant worrying very much.

Suddenly, a glowing love letter with a book addressed to me arrived in our new apartment. Polli and I wondered where Keil had gotten our address in Nuremberg. Could it be our younger sister Brigitte again?

The letter read:

> *"Dear, lovely Hertha,*
>
> *I waited patiently four long years to finally write this letter to you. I saw you from the distance at the railroad station in Solnhofen, last time you came home. You grew up and became a beautiful young woman. I love you more than ever, and hope you won't turn me away again.*
> *I admire your thoughts about the world we live in and what you like to do. You were a marvelous girl then, and I'm sure you still are today.*
> *You are my angel, my great and only love in my life. To better understand me and my love for you, I ask you to please read the book I am sending you with my letter. I hope you like the book "Die Heilige und ihr Narr". It is a romance about a love-crazy man and a saintly woman.*
> *I count the minutes till I hear from you and hope so much we can see each other soon.*
>
> *Your great admirer and lover,*
>
> *Fritz Keil"*

In another letter, he wrote about his deep dislike for my sister Polli and described her as a person who, out of selfish interests, tried to influence me against him. Keil claimed and accused Polli trying to put a wedge between me and him. In stark contrast to the admiration he felt for me, he threatened Polli in his letter: *"If you don't stop intervening, I'll kill you,*

you jealous devilish girl, who doesn't have her sister's best interest in mind." Nothing of the sort was true. After this accusation Polli and I thought the man had become crazy.

"What nerve that Keil has to threaten me," Polli protested angrily over his letters and even more over his threat to kill her. "I'll go to the police, this is too much. This man is dangerous." Scared, we asked our grandmother to come and live with us for a while, protecting her on her way to work. We decided I had to talk to Keil before we would involve the police. With great uneasiness, I sent him a letter asking for a meeting to talk things over.

A week later, Keil stood in front of our apartment door with hopeful, loving eyes. Putting all my strength together, I told him, "I am not the person you imagine I am, and I don't love you. I never did love you. Please stop sending me any more letters and don't try to see me again." It was a difficult task, telling this man to stop bothering us and let my sister and me live in peace.

"You are still so young," he said. "Maybe with time you could learn to love me. I can wait and hope. I will always love you, no matter what happens."

Nothing I could say nor do would convince Keil to not think of me as his beautiful angel. Books and letters kept coming by mail, and I sent them all back. This went on for several months until I threatened him to call the police. Then, he sent a final letter with this poem:

Good Bye My Love

I bear no grudge, even though my heart is breaking!
Love lost forever! I bear no grudge.
Although you shine in diamond splendor,
No beam falls into the night of your heart.
I bear no grudge, even though my heart is breaking.

Fifty years later, my sister Brigitte heard from Keil's former cleaning woman, that he never married and claimed I was his only, his greatest love; and in his living room hung an oil painting of his 'angel Hertha' for many decades.

Fritz Keil died in December 2010 in Weissenburg, from a fall on the ice, after three weeks in a coma.

32

Lessons of Life

In March 1953, barely seventeen years old, Polli and I left home. We had finished business-college and accepted job offers in the accounting department of Photo Porst in Nuremburg.

The company was well known and claimed to be the world's biggest photo enterprise. Its founder and CEO, Hans Porst, had access to money in a Swiss bank and founded his photo business in 1948, right after the German currency reform when it was difficult to get loans. He was a man of vision, originating the first mail-order house for photographic equipment and thereby selling cameras and accessories worldwide. He became a millionaire within a few years after he started his business.

Polli and I lived with Tante (Aunt) Paula and her son in an apartment in Moegeldorf, a suburb of Nuremberg. Every day, we walked thirty minutes along the Pegnitz River to work. Onkel (Uncle) Paul, Tante Paula's husband, had died a few months earlier, and Tante Paula had the space to accommodate us. She was very fond of us, and our closeness helped her getting over the mourning of her husband's death. Mother was happy about this arrangement, too, as it meant not to have her two girls living alone in the big city.

Tante Paula, who was our grandmother's sister, had lived with us in Solnhofen during the war. Her son Guenter was her late and only child. Guenter was a colorless, thin and timid boy of thirteen whose bad luck was, to be born to two elderly, overprotective parents.

Tante Paula was now our guardian and took her job very seriously. She worried when we didn't come home at the exact appointed time after work. She worried when we went out to a movie at night. She was upset when we were late for evening supper. Polli and I were used to a lot of freedom at home. It was not easy for us to be subjected to Tante Paula's constant worrying. But we appreciated Tante Paula's offer to stay with her, knowing how difficult it was to find any rooms or apartments in Nuremberg as so many buildings were still in ruins from the war.

At the age of sixty, Tante Paula was still a good-looking, slender woman with black, slightly graying hair, combed back and tied in a knot. She had warm, dark brown eyes and exquisitely fine features.

However, good-hearted Tante Paula was a bundle of nerves, easily upset and forgetful. We girls found her always searching for her keys. Sometimes she spent hours looking for a single key and asked us twins to help her in her search. Tante Paula also had the habit of locking doors, drawers and cabinets, even the little pantry with hardly any food in it.

"Tante Paula, you said you trust us. So why do you lock things up?" we asked her. "Oh, I don't know! I am so used to doing it since the war when nothing was safe."

When Tante Paula wasn't worrying about something, we all had a great time. We took long walks together in the pinewoods near Moegeldorf and the *'Tiergarten'* (Animal Park). She showed us the ruins of the once-beautiful inner city of Nuremberg, heavily bombed in air raids in 1943 and 1944. The old city, famous since the Middle-Ages, was 90% destroyed and only partly rebuilt. The former old city character had yet to be restored. The restrictive building codes resulted in new building activities on the outskirts and a vast, empty inner city.

Polli and I were glad we had a place to stay, while getting used to our first job. We were employed in the accounting department at Photo Porst's large, four-story main building. My office was a floor above Polli's. My stern boss and our department head, about fifty years old, never smiled. Accordingly, my six colleagues didn't smile either. In contrast to my office, the people in Polli's office had little lunch parties filled with fun and laughter. Naturally, I tried to spend my free time with Polli's group whenever I could.

Photo Porst allowed customers to make monthly installment payments. We employees had to catch the lazy customers or the intentionally forgetful and remind them of their payments due. My worst customer was Pete Seeger, the American folksinger. He returned to the USA after he bought several thousand dollars worth of merchandise on the installment plan. He never answered my letters, nor did he pay.

Polli and I worked in a comfortable and modern environment among seven hundred employees. In the first years of the company, Hans Porst, the president of the company, treated his employees very well. He tried to keep his people happy with all kinds of incentives. His business philosophy was: Happy employees are good workers. Photo Porst offered company vacations and ski-trips to Austria at reduced cost. Most of the time, Mr. Porst joined his employees at company picnics, parties and dinners on weekends. At these activities, we employees called our enjoyable boss "Onkel Hans".

Polli and I bought our first camera, a used "Retina", and took free photo and photo lab courses at Porst's city office. Soon we became enthusiastic photographers and went on the lookout for best pictures to send in for the monthly Photo Magazine competition.

Once, while walking home along the river Pegnitz on a cold day in February, Polli suddenly stopped and shouted!

"Look over there, Hertha! Look at the view! This could become the most beautiful photo of our picture collection!" While she was talking, she went over to the edge of the partly frozen river and bent down on her knees to get a better view. I followed her, also bending down to see what she was looking at. Excitedly, we discussed the different angles to get the best picture of an old church and its tower, bathed in the reddish-golden evening sunlight. The image reflected in the water and the ice we were standing on.

Suddenly the ice cracked under Polli's feet, and she started sliding towards the open water. I tried to grab her and also started sliding. In the next moment, we were both waist deep in the ice-cold water. Frantically looking around, we didn't see a way to climb out. Our worries changed into panic as we tried repeatedly to get out of the water by lifting one another up, but all efforts failed.

After what seemed an endless time, we heard a bicycle on the gravel path nearby. We screamed for help as loud as we could. A minute later, a face appeared at the edge of the ice with big eyes full of surprise. "Incredible! Incredible," we heard the person call out, laughing heartily and coughing at the same time. We, down in the cold water, didn't think it was funny. "Save us! We can't get out by ourselves! Help us!" Polli and I called up to the strange face, begging to be rescued. Yet the face disappeared without a word. To us worrying and freezing twins in the water, its absence felt like forever. Finally, the man came back with a rope and, while lying down on the ice, he threw us one end of the rope. "You go first, Hertha!" Polli commanded. With numb fingers, I held on to the rope, while the man pulled me out onto the ice just a few feet from its edge. A minute later he pulled Polly to safety. Shivering, we thanked the man that had saved our lives.

"Don't waste time thanking me!" he said, motioning over to the walkway. "Run! Just run home before you catch pneumonia!" Still laughing and shaking his head, the stranger got on his bike and rode off.

Polli and I ran as fast as we could towards Moegeldorf. With every step we took, our knitted woolen skirts became longer and heavier with the ice jingling on the seams and the water squeaking in our boots. We didn't worry about the wet camera any more, we just ran home.

"Oh, my God," Tante Paula screamed when she opened the door. "What happened to you? Did you fall off the bridge?"

Polli and I squeezed into Tante Paula's old-fashioned bathtub and slowly defrosted in the warm water. Afterwards, holding a cup of hot chamomile tea in our hands, we eagerly told her about our accident. Surprisingly, we never became ill or got a cold from that icy experience.

Half a year later, Polli and I moved into our own, newly built Photo Porst apartment. Since affordable places to live were still very difficult to find in the city, Hans Porst used the situation to his advantage. By renting the apartments only to his preferred employees, he provided incentives and tied the good workers to his company. We were so happy to have our own little place. Excitedly, we spent weeks looking for furniture we could afford. Proud of our new home, we often invited Tante Paula and Guenter for dinner on Sundays.

One day we twins were asked if we would like to pose together for the monthly Photo Porst Magazine which was sent to customers all around the world. We had no objection making some extra money to pay for our new furniture. The photo appeared on the front cover of the magazine. Underneath the photo it said in big letters *"Pretty Photo Porst Twins."* We were shocked when, only a few days after the magazine was published, we received a flood of letters from Photo Porst customers. Without our knowledge or consent, our address had been listed on the inside of the cover page. Polli and I didn't like it, having our names and address known to so many people. But it was done and it couldn't be changed any more. After our complaint at the personnel office, we received a small payment raise and more offers for photo sessions.

Mr. Porst was a shrewd businessman and expected a lot from his employees by having them compete against one another. He kept good employees in the company by giving raises and extra opportunities, but he used them and their talents for his business *and* private purposes. Occasionally, Polly and I had to dress as maids and serve at private parties in his luxurious villa.

Among the many letters we received from the magazine publication, most written in English, we answered six to practice our rusty school English. Polli wrote to someone in India, Saudi Arabia and Kenya. I corresponded with a Danish photographer, an archeologist digging in Celtic ruins in Ireland, and somebody else I don't remember. However, I lost interest and stopped writing after a short while. Polli did the same a few months later. We had mixed feelings about being known as *The Photo Porst Twins* after being portrayed again in several company magazines.

The Photo Porst Twins

Several months later, we received a telephone call from the famous talk show host, Fred Rauch, who offered us a part in a fashion show in Nuremberg. Intrigued and flattered by the offer, we accepted. However, we obviously were not trained fashion models like some of the former beauty queens in the show. With their beautifully made up faces and expensive dresses they looked down upon us. During the show, we found out we were used only once as a surprise effect for the audience in the fashion show quiz.

Polli walked out onto the stage in a stunning evening gown. A few moments after she disappeared behind the curtain, she-so it appeared, but in truth it was I-came out in a different dress to the disbelief and laughter of the audience. Spectators were to guess how it was possible, for a model to change into another dress in just a few seconds.

Feeling disappointed and deceived, Polli and I declined to participate in the next fashion show. Fred Rauch, a man in his fifties with graying hair, invited us to an exclusive restaurant, trying to make up for not telling us beforehand what we had been expected to do in the fashion show. He succeeded persuading us to come to the next fashion show. His real intentions, however, became clear to us when he wanted to come up to our apartment after he brought us home.

In spite of these few negative experiences, Polli and I enjoyed living in Nuremberg with its cultural offerings and pretty surrounding countryside. We also appreciated our apartment and our independence. Having grown up in the sheltered environment of a small town, we learned quickly that life in a big city was quite different. Being shy young twins, we were more exposed to the dangers of big city life and to people trying to take advantage of us, like Hans Porst and Fred Rauch.

Our experiences during these years as the *Photo Porst Twins* made us grow up faster and taught us some lessons for life. Lessons we would never forget.

33

Falling in Love

In the mid-fifties, '*Fasching*' (Carnival) was the time for fun and amusement. People went to costume parties, big ballroom dances and colorful parades, similar to those at Carnival in New Orleans. The country's economy had recovered and young folks liked to enjoy themselves after the dreary years following World War II.

Polli and I were just eighteen years old when good friends of Mother's invited us to a costume ball during carnival in Solnhofen. When our mother made some pretty costumes for us to wear, we twins were all excited to go to our first '*Faschingsball*'. I was dressed as a Spanish flamenco dancer and Polli as an Arabian harem girl. Polli won first prize in the competition for best costume that evening. Fritz went to the ball with a friend and, as soon as he had seen us twins, he came over to our table and asked me for a dance. I was so surprised at his changed and friendly behavior, I forgot the new dance steps I had learned a few weeks earlier. I was embarrassed for my bad dancing.

At 'Faschingsball' with Fritz

Several weeks later, Mrs. Will asked us whether Polli and I would like to come over to their house after dinner on one of the weekends her son Fritz was home from Munich. He would love to show us some new dances. She added, "He is a very good dancer and knows all the new ballroom dances. Fritz watches the International Dance Tournament in Munich every year."

We hesitated, but Mrs. Will was so excited, hinting with a twinkle in her eyes, "I wonder if Fritz can tell the two of you apart?"

With mixed feelings, we came at the appointed time on Saturday evening. Mrs. Will and her son Fritz had just finished their dinner when we arrived. "Oh, are we too early? We don't like to intrude and can come back later." Polli said, turning towards the door. Mrs. Will rose from her chair and said, "Oh, no, don't go. I'm sorry we are late with dinner. Please come in and join Fritz and me for dessert."

Later that evening in the big living room, we all had fun listening to records of the newest ballroom dance music. Fritz was an excellent teacher and took turns showing us girls the new steps. Polli and I enjoyed getting a free dance lesson, and Mrs. Will was eager to test her son whether he could tell the twins apart. She asked him to get her a glass of water from the kitchen.

Excited about her practical joke, she dimmed the lights a little and asked us girls to change our seats. Since Fritz alternated in asking us to dance, he danced with Polli twice in a row, although it would have been my turn to dance with him. But a short while after starting to dance with Polli, Fritz calmly remarked: "So, you three played a little trick on me, didn't you? This is Polli, I am dancing with, not Hertha!"

"How did you know? I can't tell them apart, and I see them both so often." Mrs. Will asked, disappointed.

Who is Who: Hertha and Polli

"Oh," Fritz replied wistfully," I danced with Hertha several weeks ago at the '*Faschingsball*'. I can't tell them apart when I see them on the streets, but I *can* tell when dancing with them."

Ever since then, I loved to dance the Tango, the Rumba, the Foxtrot and the Waltz. It was that evening, when dancing the Tango with Fritz, when I think I fell in love with that self-assured, good-looking young man.

Fritz was a slender, spirited and sporty twenty-three year old, with curly, blond hair and brown eyes. His charming personality, straight posture and a certain air of learned importance never missed to impress me every time I saw him. All of a sudden, I was smitten by this young man, and didn't dare to reveal my feelings to anyone, except my sister Polly.

Sometimes on our weekend walks with Mrs. Will, when Fritz had come home from Munich, he joined us, and my heart jubilated and worried at the same time. Hurting when I had to listen to him talking excitedly about his friends and the girls he danced with at the Regina Hotel in Munich, I could no longer enjoy the beauty of the countryside. And yet, Fritz appeared the more attractive to me, the more I tried to shun my feelings for him. Many, many months went by, and I had given up hope ever to expect love in return.

During the summer, Polli and I went with a group of young men and women from Solnhofen on a bicycle trip around Italy's gorgeous Lake Garda. We learned to like this group during this trip and accepted their invitation to a dance in Solnhofen after we returned. After dancing with one of the boys, I noticed to my surprise Fritz sitting at another table on the other side of the dance hall. He was together with a young man I didn't recognize. I had no idea Fritz was in town. Just when the next dance was about to start, Fritz and his friend were standing at our table asking Polli and me for a dance. As it was common practice for men to ask women, seated at other tables, for a dance, we accepted. Fritz danced with me, his friend with Polli. After the dance, Fritz formally introduced his friend, Rolf Guetermann, to us. He was from Switzerland and studied business at the university in Munich. We thought he was a charming and entertaining young man. So Polli did not mind dancing repeatedly with him, and I enjoyed dancing with Fritz. After the dance, we enjoyed a romantic walk by moonshine high above the town.

One Saturday afternoon, not long after the dance, Fritz caught me by surprise, when he rang our door bell and asked me whether I would like to join him on a short hike to the Teufelkanzel, a dramatic square rock used by the Celts for religious ceremonies two thousand years ago. Feeling the blood shooting into my head, I accepted. All the time, while we were walking and carrying on an animated conversation, I wondered whether he had fallen in love with me.

We had more lovely walks on some of the following weekends, and I was excited when Fritz invited Polly and me to come to Munich to go sailing on Lake Starnberg with him and his two best college friends.

In the early morning two weeks later, Polly and I took a bus to travel the 150 miles from Nuremberg to Munich. We met Fritz and his friends, both named Eberhard at the Munich railroad station on a sunny, warm day. Looking at the two Eberhards the first time I whispered to Polly, "It is so funny, but don't laugh, one of them is tall and slim and the other one short and stout. Later we had lots of laughter when we found out, Fritz had already given them the nicknames "Eberhard the Tall" and "Eberhard the Short".

Half an hour later, we arrived at Lake Starnberg and rented a small sailboat at a public marina. "Eberhard the Tall" proudly proclaimed he knew how to sail, having taken a sailing lesson a short while ago. None of us others had any experience in sailing. We all enjoyed ourselves, sailing along in light winds and having lively conversations. The three students had become best friends, having met at the university three years earlier. Happily talking, we didn't notice that the wind was slowly dying down, and we were stuck in the middle of the lake. When it became time to row ashore, we found only one paddle in the boat. We were still far away from the shore when Polli shouted, "Look there leaves our last train for Munich!"

We hitchhiked back to Munich and barely caught our bus to Nuremberg. On our two-hour ride home, Polly leaned over to my side and said in a hushed voice, "Did you see, Fritz sent long looks over to you almost the whole time while we were sailing. I think he has fallen in love with you."

34

Separation of the Twins

In the past year, the work atmosphere at Photo Porst had changed very much to our dislike. We were made to push the time clock when we started work in the morning, went out to or returned from lunch and went home in the evening. What we found even more degrading was that everyone was being timed for efficiency every hour.

The efficiency of the fastest was applied as the norm to measure everyone's performance. There was an increasing emphasis on working faster and faster even if it meant that the quality of the work was suffering. We blamed these changes on Hans Porst, Jr., Mr. Porst's son. He was an extremely ambitious and greedy young man who was only thinking about maximizing his profits, showing no compassion for his employees.

Also, we twins were less than happy with the idea of living in Nuremberg in the long run. Neither the city itself nor the Franken mentality appealed to us that much. Nuremberg and its population had an eternal inferiority complex vis-a-vis Bavaria's capital. Munich had a long tradition excelling in music and art exhibits. In addition, Munich was favored by its convenient location close to the upper Bavarian lakes and the beautiful Alps.

Being fully aware of these advantages, Polli and I had in the past year repeatedly talked about moving to Munich.

"Hertha, would you want to go ahead to Munich and look for an apartment?" Polli asked one day. I'll stay here in Nuremberg until you find a job and a place to live. One of us has to stay here, continuing to earn money and taking care of the apartment with the furniture. Both of us know it is so much harder to find any apartment in Munich than almost anywhere else. Everybody wants to live in Munich! We were so lucky to get the apartment here to rent from Photo Porst."

Actually I didn't mind being the one first moving to Munich. I was looking forward to see Fritz again, hoping to be able to see my love more often when living in the same city.

Happily, I boarded the train to Munich to start a new life. Finding a job was very difficult; finding a place to live was worse: I had no luck finding any apartment or room. Finally I found a reasonable place in a Catholic home for girls with two roommates and a curfew at ten in the evening. At almost twenty years of age I felt being treated like a teenager, and the two girls in my room acted like high school kids. How I missed Polli who understood me so well.

However, meeting Fritz on the very first weekend made up for the little disappointments of getting acquainted with a new place. Fritz was excited about my moving to Munich. He was proud to show me his beautiful Munich, the city he had come to love in the six years he had been living here. We met on each of the following weekends and always had our cameras with us. We went from place to place, from one impressive building to the next and visited one beautiful church after the other. By the end of the first month, I found myself enthusiastic about Munich and more than ever in love with Fritz.

However, I found myself anguished thinking about my future. I cherished the increasing closeness to Fritz but was frightened by what it would mean for my togetherness with Polli, my twin-sister. What about our dream and promise of always staying together? Would I really have to choose between Fritz and Polli?.

Since I arrived in Munich and saw Fritz so often, all these questions suddenly came up. My heart was pulling me one way and my conscience another. But hadn't I made the decision already before I came to Munich? Polli knew I loved Fritz and actually urged me to come here in the first place. Was she putting our twin future into my hands? Did she want *me* to make the decision? I couldn't answer these questions, nor could I make up my mind, and I was glad I didn't have to right now. I was happy whenever I saw Fritz and hoped, time would tell.

One week after my arrival, I found a job and began my employment at the Buchner Publishing House, sending out folksy plays to schools, churches and clubs all over the country. It wasn't precisely what I had hoped for, but at least it was a start. I was learning to find my way around Munich, walking or riding my bicycle to work every day. However, when walking alone, or crossing the busy, wide streets of Munich without my twin, I felt strange and lonely.

After three weeks of my unsuccessful search for an apartment, I took the train to Solnhofen to talk to my mother and Polli. We had to discuss the housing problems I faced in Munich. It was clear, there was hardly any possibility of finding a decent place to live that I could afford. The only places on the market were expensive, newly built apartments with down-payments of 40,000 Deutsch Mark or more.

Then Mother came to the rescue with a new idea: "You know I inherited an acre of pine tree woods from my father. Why don't I sell the land and get the money for the down payment. I always hoped to move back to Munich as you know. Now, together with the income of both of you girls, we finally have a chance to pay the high rent. Aren't you glad we can all live together again? What do you say to this new idea, Hertha? We solve the problem by finding us a brand new apartment."

Excitedly, Polli and I hugged our mother, rejoicing and wondering at the same time, "Oh Mother, this is great. It's perfect. We'll be a family again. But Mother, what about Bibi and Butz?" Polli asked, doubtful about this new solution.

"Don't worry, I considered it all. Your sister Bibi will stay two more years with your grandmother until she finishes high school, and your teenage brother will come to Munich with me and start an apprenticeship."

With new hope, I returned to my life in Munich, thinking it would only be another few months until we would all be together again.

During the following hot summer days in July of 1956, I spent a lot of time together with Fritz. We bicycled to the outskirts of Munich and went swimming in the cold, green Isar River. Shivering afterwards we went racing each other along the Isar banks to get warm again.

On one of Bavaria's long religious holidays, Fritz and I used this chance for a trip farther away. We rode our bicycles south to Lake Starnberg. The popular lake was too crowded for us. We saw people everywhere, swimming, canoeing, sailing or sunbathing on the few stony beaches at the shore. Too much activity at this beautiful lake for our taste, we thought. We fled to Lake Chiemsee two hours away to the southeast. Sweaty and pursued by horseflies, we dove into the water as soon we arrived at the lake, hoping to escape the dozens of insects that had been bothering us when we were riding our bikes. However, many of them followed us onto the water and stung us the minute our heads appeared above the surface.

Slapping and splashing around us didn't seem to help much. But returning home to Munich in the coolness of the evening after a hot summer day, we felt happy and envigorated.

I enjoyed long walks with Fritz in the Englische Garten, Munich's biggest park with little lakes, fast flowing streams, wide lawns and two-hundred year-old trees. One of our favorite places to visit in the park was the '*Monopterus*', a charming Greek-style gazebo.

All these activities together made us fonder of each other during those hot, humid weeks in July. There was now no question any longer: We were in love with each other.

One day in mid-July, Polli phoned me, all excited, "You can't guess who visited me yesterday! I tell you, what a surprise! It was a visit from Ashraf Abou Chamat. You remember the Syrian man, living in Saudi Arabia who wrote to me in such a funny Berlin dialect? I had stopped corresponding with him and the others from the Porst magazine shortly after you did and forgot all about this guy. Now he stood in front of my door!"

"But Polli, you didn't let him in?"

"Sure I did. He came all the way from Saudi Arabia to see me. He also plans to buy machines in Germany for a new company he is starting together with a Palestinian fellow. Ashraf also has to visit the Siemens Company in Berlin. He is a liaison officer for the company in Riyadh. Oh Hertha, I tell you, he is such a nice, good-looking man, and so charming!"

I was shocked and speechless. My sister, always the wiser of us twins, suddenly being on fire, blinded by love, or whatever it was. I had to warn her, remind her about the funny first letters this man wrote to Polli. They turned out to have been written by his German friend, as he later admitted. I wondered what else wasn't true, if a letter was his bait under false pretenses.

Polli wouldn't listen to any warnings I gave her, nor would she consider Mother's intense worries of a relationship with an Arab. She was swept away by the charms of this man. Excited as I never heard her before, Polli confided to me on the phone, "Hertha, you can't imagine how happy I am. I am so much in love. Everything is so wonderful, like in a dream. Hertha please don't worry. Be happy with me and Ashraf."

Two weeks later, after completing his business obligations, Ashraf visited our mother in Solnhofen to ask for Polli's hand, and the next day

I received a phone call from him asking me to meet him in the ice cream parlor Rialto at Karlsplatz.

Ashraf was a tall, well-built man with a high forehead, a prominent nose, and an open, friendly face. He was about fifteen years older than Polli. His features seemed to me more Armenian than Arabic. Ashraf told me with pride and a chuckle, "I won the Mr. Berlin competition a few years ago and as you can see, I am keeping in shape". When I asked him about his religion he claimed he was neither Moslem nor Christian, but an atheist. "I became a Communist while studying in Paris as a young man. Religions are made to have power over the people," Ashraf explained with a strong conviction in his voice.

Changing the subject, Ashraf told me about his and Polli's engagement plan. He said he was in love with Polli for her good-heartedness, charm and beauty. Seeing my hesitation, Aschraf assured me in a tone of indignation, "Don't worry, I have money, and I promise you, I'll be a loving husband and give Polli a good and interesting life." He told me, they planned to celebrate their engagement in Catholica, Italy or in Rome. With pride in his gleaming black eyes, he stated proudly, "My relatives in Damascus are prominent families, and my brother is the Syrian Minister of Agriculture. You should also know, my nieces are about the same age as Polli, and they will help her to adjust to life in Syria."

Shocked over the sudden turn of events, I couldn't understand my sister's actions. I wished Polli all the happiness in the world, but this was too sudden, too strange a turn of events. However, for all my questions and worries, charming Ashraf had a perfect answer.

For many days after my meeting with Ashraf, I felt paralyzed. I spent the hours in a daze. How could she do that to me, to herself? I couldn't understand.

Then I received a second shock: Mother had trouble selling the land. The trees had a disease and needed to be sprayed and checked by the state authorities. She could not move to Munich for many months.

When fall came, Fritz had to work on his master thesis, and I offered to type his fifty page long thesis in the evenings and on some weekends. But we still found time to go out. We both enjoyed the many activities, museums and theaters in the city, and Fritz found ever-new places I hadn't seen before. I grew to like the city with its beautiful buildings, its culture and the atmosphere of big city life. With time I learned to admire Fritz. Besides his full-time studies, he sold newspapers in the evening to make money for his living expenses. Fortunately, a scholarship paid for the university tuition and fees. Although he had little money, he always found ways to pay for concerts or the theater and to enjoy trips to the countryside. I realized we had a lot in common: An interest in classical music and the arts, but also in dancing, sports and the outdoors.

In the meantime, Polli sent me postcards from Catholica, Rome and Damascus with descriptions of life in Syria. But there was little information about her personal life, and I kept wondering, what happened to my twin who used to tell me everything.

Several months later, one of her few letters described the marvelous old city of Damascus, the bazaar, where she could only go with a male relative of Ashraf's; and how she learned cooking Syrian dishes from his sister. Ashraf had to return to his job in Riyadh, and Polli stayed with his relatives in Syria. No one there knew any German or English; only a few of the young cousins spoke some French. But Polli couldn't understand them. Her life must have been difficult, living among so many strangers in a very different society. However, Polli never complained. I knew Polli was very adaptable to new and different circumstances.

In another letter, Polli described the pampered life of the women in Ashraf's family: They ordered their formal dresses from the fashion designers in Paris, and didn't do any work. These fine ladies seemed to be happy socializing among each other and raising their families. I could see how infatuated my sister had become with all the glamour of their lifestyle.

But I couldn't help wondering whether everything was all right and her adventure was not heading for trouble. Polli's happiness and future in this totally different society seemed to me quite questionable.

Polli had not married yet. The wedding was planned to take place in Damascus later in the year. In a last attempt to have Polli consider my concerns, I wrote her a letter begging her to come back to me and our family. After weeks of silence passed and I didn't hear from her I knew Polli had made up her mind to stay.

Three days after our twenty-first birthday Polli married Ashraf and moved with him to Riadh, Saudi Arabia.

I realized then that our love of two men, however different they were, was stronger than our dreams and promises to stay together as twins forever.

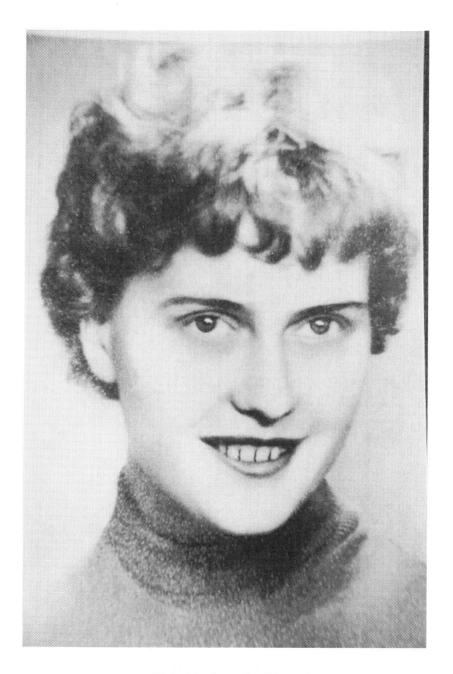

Twin Hertha at Age Twenty

Postscript

The time when we identical twins fell in love with the men of our dreams now lies more than fifty years in the past.

Polli married a Syrian businessman when she was twenty-one years old. She lived in the Near East for five years and then came to live with her husband and two children in Munich, the city where she was born. Her husband passed away three years ago.

I married a German physicist one and a half years later and followed my husband to live in the United States, originally planning to stay for two years, which became twenty years and then fifty years. After having made our home in Schenectady, New York for thirty years, we moved west to Salt Lake City, Utah for several years and then on to California. We now live in Santa Barbara, California and our three children in Albany, NY, Los Angeles and Salt Lake City.

In spite of us twins living six thousand miles apart; being married to husbands with totally different personalities and heritage; having different lifestyles; and being exposed to significantly different societal environments, Polli and I have maintained a very close relationship. In the last decade alone, we have visited each other every year for several months. Every time we meet again after a year, we feel as though we had seen each other the day before. The love and warmth, the deep mutual understanding and compassion are back in an instant.

I am happy and grateful for having grown up together with my identical twin and for being able to enjoy a continued close relationship with her later in life.